1400 Bible Facts: A Quiz Book

1400 Bible Facts:
A Quiz Book

E. C. McKenzie

BAKER BOOK HOUSE
Grand Rapids, Michigan

Formerly published under the title,
It's In the Bible Quiz Book

© 1959 by Baker Book House Company

ISBN: 0-8010-5965-8

Fifth printing, September 1982

PHOTOLITHOPRINTED BY CUSHING - MALLOY, INC.
ANN ARBOR, MICHIGAN, UNITED STATES OF AMERICA

PREFACE

The contents of this book are what its title indicates — nothing more. These interesting bits of Biblical information, presented in question and answer form, have been gleaned from many sources over a period of more than twenty-five years. No claim is made to complete originality.

The Bible is the most human book in the world, a fact which the average Bible student has overlooked. It speaks the truth about both friend and foe. It portrays its heroes to us at their best and at their worst. The everyday experiences of these heroes are as varied, fascinating, heartbreaking, and disappointing as are our own experiences.

For many years I have carefully and prayerfully studied the Bible with the purpose of identifying its fundamentals and essentials. While making this search for spiritual truths, I found a great number of odd, strange, and interesting things in the text of our English Bible. I also found in the lives of Bible men and women many unique and sometimes laughable incidents and events which reveal them to us as real human beings. My efforts to collect these "facts" have proved a delightful hobby for me. I now pass them on to you for your personal enjoyment and amusement.

If the reading of this book should encourage and inspire you to a more serious study of the Bible, I shall feel amply rewarded for my efforts.

E. C. McKenzie

TO MY GRANDCHIDREN
JEANIE AND KEN

1. How many times did Jesus become angry?
2. Can an angel keep a secret?
3. Does the Bible explain how butter is made?
4. What was the first command that God gave to man?
5. How many commandments are recorded in the Old Testament?
6. What was the first change of style in clothing?
7. Which is longer, the shortest chapter in the Bible or the longest verse in the Bible?
8. What is the Bible remedy for boils?
9. Does a mule possess understanding?
10. The names of how many Bible women are spelled the same backwards and forwards?
11. Was it prophesied that the Lord would shave with a razor?
12. Who was the father of his own grandchildren?
13. How many perfect men are mentioned by name in the Scriptures?
14. Does the Bible give a formula for achieving prosperity and success?
15. What boy became a father when he was eleven years old?
16. What is the Bible penalty for kidnapping?
17. Who was the first woman to use cosmetics?
18. Was Noah a woman?
19. Which book of the Bible has the initials S. O. S.?
20. Where is it recorded that meal was once used to counteract poison?
21. Did Jesus ever use the word *religion?*
22. Does the Bible refer to a dead man who is still speaking?
23. How many times must a Christian forgive a sinful brother?
24. In olden times, could left-handed people throw more accurately than those who were right-handed?

25. During the days of King Solomon, which cost more, a horse or a chariot?
26. Which is the middle verse of the Bible?
27. Did Moses marry a colored woman?
28. How many sheep did Job have on his ranch?
29. Is there a recipe in the Bible for making friends?
30. Where in the Scriptures is it recorded that God hates seven things?
31. Is there a prophetic description of the automobile in the Bible?
32. Was there ever a time when everybody in the world was filthy?
33. Does the Bible say that Cain met and married his wife in the land of Nod?
34. Were cowards exempt from military service in the Jewish army?
35. Which are mentioned first in the Bible, horses or mules?
36. Is it true that Eve's name was also Adam?
37. How many words does the Bible contain?
38. How many men were killed because they could not pronounce a certain word correctly?
39. Which is the middle verse of the Old Testament?
40. In the Bible, what is the big toe called?
41. Were the early Jewish women forbidden to wear men's clothing?
42. Which is the only chapter in the Bible that ends with a comma?
43. Who was King Rehoboam's favorite wife?
44. Which Old Testament king installed a waterworks system in Jerusalem?
45. Is the word *Bible* in the Bible?
46. Where is it recorded that salt was once used to purify drinking water?
47. Are any of the original writings of the Apostles now in existence?
48. What woman was described as having been "fair and beautiful" when she was a girl?
49. Who requested that his tears be put in God's bottle?

50. Of whom did God say, "there is none like him"?
51. Does the Bible teach that the human family must earn its bread by the "sweat of the brow"?
52. Who once commanded that the Apostle Paul be smitten on the mouth?
53. Which is the only domestic animal not mentioned in the Bible?
54. How many letters does the Bible contain?
55. Upon whom did God pronounce the first curse?
56. What man of the New Testament admitted he "sabatoged" the church of God?
57. Where is it recorded that an iron ax swam?
58. Is it true that a "sissy" (effeminate) cannot inherit the kingdom of God?
59. How many verses does the Bible contain?
60. What is the specified time required to raise the dead?
61. Do the Scriptures seem to indicate that the poor sleep better than the wealthy?
62. What kind of women caused King Solomon to sin?
63. Who erected a tombstone at the grave of his wife?
64. Where is the information that a certain woman boiled and ate her son?
65. What famous father and son were circumcised the same day?
66. Who stated publicly that God "liked him"?
67. What is the longest word in the Bible?
68. With what are Christians commanded to season their talk?
69. What prominent New Testament character once ate with the hogs?
70. What prominent man of the Old Testament married his half-sister?
71. How many times is the word *eternity* mentioned in the Scriptures?
72. What was the relationship of Huz and Buz?
73. Were the early Jews forbidden to eat pork?

11

74. In which chapter of the Bible does each verse end with the words, "for his mercy endureth forever"?

75. What well-known husband and wife of the Old Testament were first cousins?

76. Who in the Bible is described as a "man of rest"?

77. What is the book of Acts of Apostles sometimes called?

78. When and by whom was the Bible divided into chapters?

79. Who requested God to let him alone so that he could take a little comfort before he died?

80. Which book in the Bible contains neither the words *Lord* nor *God?*

81. Was Jesus baptized *in* or *near* the Jordan river?

82. Into how many different languages and dialects has the Bible been translated?

83. When and by whom was the Bible divided into verses?

84. When was the entire Bible printed in English for the first time?

85. Why did the Prophet Jeremiah once rebuke the people of Israel?

86. Where in the Bible is it recorded that nine generations were living at one time?

87. Which was the first book to be printed from movable type?

88. When was the first English Bible printed in America?

89. Who was the first person to translate the entire Bible into the English language?

90. Who was warned against "meddling with God"?

91. When was the first Bible printed on India paper?

92. Where did the women of Jerusalem sometimes knead their dough?

93. What was Daniel's other name?

94. Does the Bible refer to the unclean habits of swine?

95. When was the first Bible bound with the "divinity circuit"?

96. Who was carried up to heaven by a whirlwind?

97. What woman married her brother's son?

98. Who was condemned to death for saying his prayers?

99. Is it recorded in the Scriptures that Jesus was ever sick?

100. The people of what city did not know their right hand from their left?

101. Who attempted to commit murder at a dining table?

102. Does every star in the heavens have a name?

103. Which of the Old Testament prophets once wished that he had a sword in his hand?

104. How many people are mentioned by name in the Bible?

105. Was there ever a time in the life of David when he was afraid of God?

106. Where did the Lord smite His enemies?

107. Who won his wife by slaying two hundred men?

108. When was the first Bible bound in flexible leather?

109. Who once tried to detain an angel?

110. Does the Bible contain words or names of more than six syllables?

111. What ancient nation detested shepherds?

112. What was the length of the longest drouth recorded in the Scriptures?

113. Which is the middle verse of the New Testament?

114. Who was the author of the *Golden Rule,* and where is it found in the Bible?

115. Whose anger was said to have "burned" in him?

116. Which is the shortest verse in the Old Testament?

117. How many pairs of brothers were among the Twelve Apostles?

118. Can it be proved that Jesus was a carpenter?

119. Who were the first disbelievers in the resurrection of Christ?

120. How many sacred books are mentioned in the Bible but are not included in it?

121. Who once asked for a drink of water but was given milk instead?

122. What was the punishment for pre-marital infidelity among the early Jews?

123. In which chapter of the Bible are there four verses which read exactly alike?

124. Was there ever a time when everybody in Moab was bald-headed?

125. According to the Bible, how many people are a few?

126. Which is the middle book of the Old Testament?

127. Where in the Bible is it recorded that Adam named his wife?

128. Is it true that the deathday of a person is better than his birth-day?

129. Who kissed a beautiful girl and then wept?

130. What man removed one of his shoes to bind a contract?

131. What was the only question Jesus ever asked His Father?

132. Does the Bible make mention of a man turning a dish upside down after he wipes it?

133. In Old Testament times, what was the fine for slandering a virgin?

134. Who was Hen?

135. What man sat down under a juniper tree and prayed to die?

136. What place was said to have been a Sabbath day's journey from Jerusalem?

137. Who described himself as being "old and gray-headed?

138. What is the shortest time on record for acquiring ability to speak in a foreign language?

139. What kind of people are said to have no peace?

140. Who is the only person mentioned in the Scriptures as having used a towel?

141. What was the name of David's mother?

142. According to the law of Moses, when were laborers to be paid their wages?

143. Where in the Bible is a wife described as a "good thing"?

144. Who prophesied that seven women would desire to wear the same name?

145. What was used in saving the life of the Prophet Jeremiah?

146. How many times are the words *boy* and *girl* mentioned in the Scriptures?

147. Is it true that there was a time when the poor were sold for a pair of shoes?

148. Is the expression *unpardonable sin* in the Bible?

149. Who once condemned himself when he sentenced another?

150. Who, immediately after murdering four hundred and fifty men, fled from one angry woman?

151. What great man said he was "slow of speech, and of a slow tongue"?

152. What two famous brothers died on mountain tops?

153. How many suicides are recorded in the Bible?

154. Was there ever a war in heaven?

155. For how long did an Ephesian mob shout one sentence?

156. Who was the first person to confess Jesus as being the Son of God?

157. The inhabitants of what city were commanded to cut off their hair and throw it away?

158. How many direct quotations from the Old Testament are recorded in the New Testament?

159. What garment worn by the Prophet Jeremiah was not to be put in water?

160. What prominent man of the Old Testament owned nine hundred chariots?

161. Is there a time to die?

162. Is it possible for a person to die before his time?

163. Who once asked if there is any taste in the white of an egg?

164. Where is it recorded in the Scriptures that a certain woman asked the Prophet Elisha not to tell her a lie?

165. Upon what people was consumption (tuberculosis) threatened as a punishment?

166. What is the meaning of the word *venison* as used in the Bible?

167. Who wrote a book, gave it to his friend, and told him to throw it in a certain river?

168. Did the Lord once think He would do evil to His people, but changed His mind?

169. Is it true that the words *hare* and *tortoise* are mentioned in the same chapter in the Bible?

170. When was the Red Letter New Testament first published?

171. What was Solomon's other name?

172. What is one thing that man cannot tame?

173. Are great men always wise?

174. What two Christian missionaries once had a quarrel and separated, each going his own way?

175. Why are the books of Matthew, Mark, and Luke often referred to as the synoptic gospels?

176. Which Old Testament prophet mentioned a bed that was too short and a cover that was too narrow?

177. Does the Bible mention four-footed fowl?

178. What Old Testament king had a house that was made of ivory?

179. Has the sun ever gone down at noon?

180. How are atheists classfied in the Bible?

181. What noted thief in his confession said, "I saw, I coveted, I took"?

182. Is there an instance in the Scriptures of God winking?

183. How many years were required in the building of King Solomon's temple?

184. Is it true that a certain Old Testament king is described as hunting for a flea?

185. How many times does the word *onions* occur in the Bible?

186. Who were the first to use writing pens?

187. Does the Bible say it is a shame for a man to wear long hair?

188. Where is it recorded that Jewish priests were forbidden to wear garments that caused them to sweat?

189. What Old Testament prophet mentioned a man who was met by a bear while running away from a lion?

190. How many chapters in the Bible contain as many as eighty verses each?

191. When was the first pocket reference Bible printed?

192. Who was the first to commit hari-kari?

193. Which is the middle book of the New Testament?

194. Which is the most dramatic book in the Bible?

195. Who burned a certain city and gave it to his daughter as a present?

196. What class of women did the Apostle Paul warn against drinking too much wine?

197. Is it possible to copyright the Bible?

198. Was it difficult for the early Jews to serve hot food on the Sabbath?

199. How many times is the word *backslider* mentioned in the Bible?

200. Who was the first "circuit judge" in Israel?

201. How many songs did Solomon write, and how many proverbs did he speak?

202. Does the Bible make mention of frying pans?

203. What three Old Testament kings were afflicted with insomnia?

204. How many times does the word *music* occur in the New Testament?

205. What prophet referred to Israel as a "backsliding heifer"?

206. Did the military laws of the Jews authorize a selective draft and a universal conscription?

207. Who, during his lifetime, erected a monument to his own memory?

208. Could Jesus read and write?

209. Where in the Scriptures is an idol factory described?

210. What mighty men of the Bible had faces like lions?

211. Which two chapters of the Bible are almost identical?

212. Which Old Testament king was referred to as "this son of a murderer"?

213. The hand of what man was said to have "dried up"?

214. Which Old Testament prophet became very angry because his prophecy was not fulfilled?

215. Who or what caused the Lord to fret?

216. Who prophesied that every knee in Israel would become "weak as water"?

217. How many times does the word *Easter* occur in the Scriptures?

218. How many men of the Bible were said to have worn hats?

219. Who referred to his wife as a "heifer"?

220. Are cedar chests mentioned in the Bible?

221. How many of Haman's sons were hanged on the same gallows?

222. Which of the Twelve Apostles admitted he was a "sinful man"?

223. Does the Lord ever sleep?

224. Is the word *religion* in the Old Testament?

225. When did the Jewish law require that a criminal be buried?

226. Who expressed deep regret that he could not weep day and night?

227. How many fish did the Apostle Peter catch on one of his fishing trips?

228. To what people did God give a bill of divorce?

229. What two Old Testament kings are described as having been very tall?

230. What did Job call the law of gravitation?

231. What king gave a feast that lasted six months?

232. How many people were enrolled in the world's first singing school?

233. How many kings once had a "drinking party"?

234. What great prophet prepared and served boiled beef to several people?

235. Who longed for a drink of well water, but refused it when brought to him?

236. Is the expression *Adamic sin* in the Bible?
237. Who praised the Lord upon receiving a mesage of doom?
238. Is it true that the first physicians were also embalmers?
239. How many kings were mutilated by having their great toes cut off?
240. Where is the recorded account of a certain man being stoned to death for picking up sticks on the Sabbath?
241. Has every kind of bird, beast, and serpent been tamed by man?
242. What was the only miracle performed by Jesus that is recorded by each of the four gospel writers?
243. Which is the longest book in the New Testament?
244. Which is the shortest book in the Old Testament?
245. How often is God angry with the wicked?
246. What prophet mentioned a writing pen of iron that had a diamond point?
247. Which of the Twelve Apostles did Jesus address as "Satan"?
248. Who was reproached for clapping his hands?
249. How many times is the word *Calvary* mentioned in the Bible?
250. What city was known as the "city of palm trees"?
251. Which of the Old Testament kings removed his mother from being queen because of her idolatry?
252. What three great men of the Bible were noted for their righteousness?
253. Were writing pens and ink in use during the days of the Apostle John?
254. Is it true that the end of a thing is better than its beginning?
255. What well-known man of the Old Testament feigned insanity very successfully?
256. Where in the Bible are ants referred to as people?
257. What did the Prophet Elijah see on Mount Horeb?
258. Was there ever a time in the history of the Israelites when frogs interfered with their cooking?
259. How many times is Palestine referred to as the "holy land"?

260. Who was the first man to experience deportation?
261. Which Old Testament prophet had a "noisy" heart?
262. Did Jesus have fleshly brothers?
263. Did Jesus also have sisters?
264. Who said his breath was "strange to his wife"?
265. What king of Israel did more to provoke the Lord to anger than all the other kings before him?
266. Who saw Satan fall from heaven?
267. How many thousand men were given a fish dinner with only two fishes?
268. What New Testament race of people were especially noted for their lying?
269. Is it true that Christians were commanded to kiss each other?
270. What proud father named a city for his son?
271. What did the Israelites do when they invaded the land of Moab?
272. Did Jesus recommend the bank as a safe place in which to keep one's money?
273. What means of transportation were used by ancient postmen?
274. What man of the New Testament protested against poor people being unwelcome at church services?
275. How many names are inscribed in the Bible's "Hall of Fame"?
276. Were mural paintings in existence in Old Testament days?
277. Who provoked David to take a census of Israel?
278. What two well-known men of the Old Testament cursed their birthdays?
279. Is the word *sermon* in the Bible?
280. With what did God smite the Philistines as a curse?
281. Where is the last prophecy of the Old Testament recorded?
282. Where did the saying, "head and shoulders above everybody" originate?
283. Was King Solomon familiar with the science of botany?
284. Who said his heart "melted in the midst of his bowels"?

285. What was the weight of Absalom's annual growth of hair?

286. According to Jewish law, how many witnesses were required to establish a charge?

287. What modern hat has the name of a Bible city?

288. How many instances of embalming are recorded in the Scriptures?

289. Is it true that the early Jews were forbidden to plow an ox and an ass together as a team?

290. What kind of containers were used in carrying the heads of King Ahab's seventy sons to Jezreel?

291. Is there an instance in the Bible of people burning their children as a sacrifice to their gods?

292. What army fled in confusion when a noise was heard?

293. On what mountain was a certain king slain at his own request?

294. How much did David pay for Ornan's threshing floor?

295. Who was the first shipbuilder?

296. What New Testament city was popularly supposed to produce nothing good?

297. What did the Prophet Elijah give to Elisha as a dying gift?

298. How many stalls were required for the accommodation of Solomon's horses and chariots?

299. Is it true that two Old Testament kings were driven from their dominion by a hornet?

300. Upon how many different occasions was the Jordan river miraculously crossed?

301. What ancient people were said to have been most clever in cutting down timber?

302. Are there any names in the Bible beginning with the letter "w"?

303. Which chapter in the Bible is remarkable for its beautiful description of natural history?

304. How many instances of sunstroke are recorded in the Scriptures?

305. How long did Job live after all his troubles had ended?

306. When was the first concordance to the entire Bible first printed, and by whom was it compiled?

307. How many words does the Bible use in explaining the power and strength of love?

308. Upon how many different occasions were savage beasts employed as instruments of God?

309. Was a Jewish priest permitted to marry a widow?

310. Where was the prophet Jeremiah told to hide his linen girdle?

311. What Old Testament words did Jesus repeat while dying on the cross?

312. What seven brothers were hanged because of their father's perfidy?

313. In olden times, did the people believe the earth was flat?

314. Where in the Bible is it recorded that fifty thousand camels were captured in war?

315. Where is the "Apostolic Benediction" recorded in the New Testament?

316. How many times does the word *Lord* occur in the Scriptures?

317. Which is the shortest chapter in the Bible?

318. Is it true that Noah Webster, author of the famous Webster's Dictionary, made a translation of the Bible?

319. In point of length, how many letters does the average word of the Bible contain?

320. According to Jewish law, was a man required to work during the first year of his married life?

321. How many miracles performed by Jesus were miracles of creation?

322. Who is the only person described in the Bible as having "paid his fare"?

323. Where is it recorded that rain once fell so heavily in Jerusalem that the people trembled and could not stand out of doors?

324. Who was the first man to be hanged?

325. What ancient people raised horses that were swifter than leopards?

326. Was there ever a time in the history of Judah when every man was conscripted for labor?

327. The voice of what man was said to have been the voice of a god?

328. What four "little things" were described as having been "exceeding wise"?

329. Who is the only woman the Bible bids us remember?

330. What penalty did Rechab and Baanah suffer for cutting off a man's hand?

331. What woman of the Old Testament made a "dummy" and put it in a bed to represent her husband ?

332. Did the Apostle Paul write a letter to the church in Corinth that has been lost?

333. Is the phrase *second coming of Christ* in the Bible?

334. Was it ever recommended that two people sleep in the same bed?

335. Was there formerly a time when it was customary for men to grasp each other's beards instead of shaking hands?

336. Where is it recorded that God once threatened horses with blindness?

337. Which seed did Jesus say was the least of all seeds?

338. The name of what man occurs most frequently in the Scriptures?

339. When does a will or testament become effective?

340. What great religious leader accused certain people of being "witnesses against themselves"?

341. What is the longest name of a place mentioned in the Bible?

342. Which is the only book in the Bible that is addressed to a woman?

343. When was the first Indian Bible printed?

344. Did God once give Moses a formula for compounding an oil for furniture?
345. Who described the Lord as riding upon a cloud?
346. Where is the recorded instance of a storm that lasted a fortnight?
347. Who died the first natural death, and at what age?
348. What man wore a complete linen ensemble?
349. Is there something similar to artificial respiration alluded to in the Scriptures?
350. Where is mention made of hail stones weighing more than one hundred pounds?
351. Who was the first Hebrew mentioned by name in the Bible?
352. What well-beloved man of the Old Testament was sold for twenty pieces of silver?
353. Who prophesied that kings would act as nursing fathers?
354. What is the oldest Bible city still in existence?
355. What Old Testament king offered forty camel loads of presents for a cure for his disease?
356. Is it true that every one attending a certain false-worship service was slain?
357. Where in the Scriptures is it recorded that a false prophet died a few months after a true prophet had foretold his death?
358. When was the first complete Japanese Bible printed in America?
359. What women in early Bible times wore a "stomacher"?
360. Who is the only man described in the Bible as having climbed a tree?
361. What prophet confessed that his "cogitations" troubled him?
362. What Old Testament mother made a fur collar and mittens for her son?
363. How many thousand chosen men were slain in one Old Testament battle?
364. How long did two light meals last the Prophet Elijah?

365. Was Jesus popular in His "home town" after He became a public teacher?

366. Is it true that the Old Testament ends with a curse, and the New Testament with a blessing?

367. Who were the only two men of the Bible described as threshing wheat?

368. Which verse in the Bible tells of a hungry man who dreams he is eating, and a thirsty man who dreams he is drinking?

369. How many times does the phrase *It is written* occur in the New Testament?

370. Which books of the Bible tell of the birth, life, death, resurrection and ascension of Christ?

371. Did Jesus have the appearance of a Jew to the extent He could be recognized as such?

372. Who was scornfully described as but a "noise"?

373. Which is the shortest verse in the Bible?

374. Was there ever a time when the people of Jerusalem could not blush?

375. When was the first Bible printed in America in the Indian language?

376. What State in the United States compares in shape and size to the country of Palestine?

377. Which of the New Testament writers referred to a wife as the "weaker vessel"?

378. Is the old saying, "escaped with the skin of the teeth," in the Bible?

379. How many wives and concubines did King Solomon have?

380. How many promises does the Bible contain?

381. Who expressed a desire that his words be written and printed in a book?

382. Are the words *ha, ha,* in the Bible?

383. Where is it recorded that a certain woman, while asleep, smothered her infant to death?

384. Is there an allusion to the science of anthropology in the Bible?

385. Who prayed while inside a fish?

386. Which verse in the Bible contains all the letters of the alphabet except "q"?

387. What was the "chained Bible"?

388. What is said to be the *Golden Text* of the Bible?

389. Are the telephone, telegraph, and radio prophesied in the Bible?

390. Who was the first city builder?

391. Was angels' food ever eaten by man?

392. Which of the Old Testament prophets believed the earth to be round?

393. Who or what is described in the Bible as the "battle ax" of God?

394. What are said to be the most sublime words in the Bible?

395. Upon a certain occasion, how many men lost their lives as a result of their curiosity?

396. Does the Bible forbid tattooing?

397. Is the expression *get religion* in the Bible?

398. Which verse in the Bible contains all the letters of the alphabet except "j"?

399. How high was the idol that King Nebuchadnezzar built?

400. Did the Negro race originate at the time God "set a mark upon Cain"? (Genesis 4:15)

401. In what way did Solomon say a child should be trained?

402. Who held up his brother's hand so that a battle might be won?

403. Whose two sons loved money and took bribes?

404. What beloved woman of the Old Testament became the mother of the world's first twins?

405. Who said that God had poured him out like milk and curdled him like cheese?

406. Who made the statement, "all that a man hath will he give for his life"?
407. Sodom was destroyed for the lack of how many righteous people?
408. Who had six fingers on each hand and six toes on each foot?
409. How many times did Jesus marvel?
410. Who said a living dog is better than a dead lion?
411. Which Old Testament prophet once conducted a "praying contest"?
412. How many men went on a *hunger strike* during the days of the Apostle Paul?
413. Is the word *beatitudes* in the Bible?
414. Was David a fearless man?
415. Was Christ ever referred to as an Apostle?
416. What well-known prophet once plowed with a twelve-yoke team of oxen?
417. Where is it recorded in the Bible that the price of a dog was not to be brought into the house of God?
418. Did any of the writers of the Bible seem to advocate the principles of life insurance?
419. Who once prophesied a paper shortage?
420. What man of the Old Testament had a pain that was perpetual and a wound that was incurable?
421. Is there ever a time when a fool is wise?
422. How deep were the quails that once filled the camp of the Israelites?
423. Did Christ really become lost when He was twelve years old?
424. How many times is the expression *breach of promise* mentioned in the Scriptures?
425. How did the Jews in the early days obtain money with which to pay their taxes?
426. How many years was the life of Hezekiah lengthened as a result of prayer ?

427. Where is the longest recorded prayer in the Bible?

428. Who suffered the humiliating experience of having his head caught in the limbs of a tree while riding upon a mule?

429. Which of the Twelve Apostles were called "sons of thunder"?

430. Is it true that David was never charged with but one sin during his entire lifetime?

431. Who massacred all the men of a city to avenge their sister's honor?

432. How many times was David called the "psalmist" in the Bible?

433. Were the early Jews forbidden to charge poor people interest on borrowed money?

434. Were the sacred singers in the Jewish temple employed full time or part time?

435. What words did Job use in referring to the grave?

436. How many women are mentioned by name as having lived before the flood?

437. Is there a verse in the Bible in which the name of Jehovah is paraphrased?

438. Which of the Apostles lived in a rented house?

439. Is there a probable allusion in the Scriptures to the destruction of the world by atomic energy?

440. How many times does the world *millennium* occur in the Bible?

441. How honest were the workmen who repaired the house of the Lord?

442. What does the Bible have to say concerning the "prodigal son"?

443. Were others, in addition to the Savior, ever called *Jesus* in the New Testament?

444. How many different times was rain sent in answer to prayer?

445. What man of the Old Testament was referred to as "this dreamer"?

446. Who once asked for money and recived something better?

447. Is a person a sinner because he sins or does he sin because he is a sinner?

448. Who once complained that he was tossed up and down like a locust?

449. Which of all the letters written to the churches by the Apostle Paul was the least doctrinal and the most personal?

450. Was there a circumstance under which a Hebrew thief could be sold into slavery?

451. Which of the Old Testament prophets alludes to the migration of birds?

452. Does the New Testament predict there shall come a time when men shall seek death but not find it?

453. How many persons does the Bible describe as having been patriarchs?

454. How many verses do the Four Gospels contain?

455. Is the word *sacrament* in the Bible?

456. Does both the Old and the New Testament warn against adding to the words of God?

457. What animal is the strongest of all beasts?

458. What was the fervent wish of Balaam?

459. Who sought retirement in a field for meditation?

460. How many times does the familiar expression *immortal soul* occur in the Scriptures?

461. Where is the only mention of a navy in the Bible?

462. What are the three most famous heads of hair mentioned in the word of God?

463. What per cent of the recorded daily conversation of Jesus was quoted literally in Old Testament verses?

464. Who sentenced ten of his concubines to life imprisonment?

465. During the great famine in Samaria, what price was paid for the head of an ass?

466. Who asked the question, "Is there anything too hard for the Lord?"

467. Which is the longest verse in the New Testament?

468. What are the first recorded words of Jesus in the New Testament?

469. Did John the Baptist ever perform a miracle?

470. In what unusual place did the children of Israel once dwell?

471. Is it true that the nearer Jesus came to the cross, the fewer were His friends?

472. Whose heart is described as being "fat as grease"?

473. What "insectivorous" man is mentioned by name in the Bible?

474. Who was the first man to wear a ring?

475. How heavy was Job's grief?

476. How many times does the word *and* occur in the New Testament?

477. What bird is most frequently mentioned in the Scriptures?

478. The eyes of what man were "put out" by his enemies?

479. What distinguished title was given to the descendants of Esau?

480. What king of Israel reigned only seven days?

481. Who are the only three persons in the Bible who names begin with the letter "F"?

482. What Old Testament king admitted he was a fool?

483. Who was the first colored man to become a Christian?

484. How many times did Jesus address the Heavenly Father as God?

485. Is the popular expression *there's nothing new under the sun* in the Bible?

486. What became of Aaron's golden calf?

487. How was the Garden of Eden watered?

488. Who named all the animals and birds of the Bible?

489. The daughters of what ruler assisted in repairing the walls of Jerusalem?

490. Who charged the Apostle Paul of writing some things which were "hard to understand"?

491. What country of the Old Testament is referred to as a "very fair heifer"?
492. Where in the Bible is the first wage contract recorded?
493. What great man of the Old Testament made soup for an angel?
494. Who were the most famous twins of Bible times?
495. What Old Testament ruler once found frogs in his bed?
496. Who was first to commit murder?
497. In what peculiar manner did Job's three friends comfort him during his illness and great sorrow?
498. What is the most noted instance of genuine friendship in the Bible?
499. What king became so jealous of another man that he "eyed" him from a certain day forward?
500. Is the airplane prophesied in the Bible?
501. In what cave did David gather four hundred guerrilla fighters?
502. What two men hid themselves in a well?
503. Is the word *benediction* in the Bible?
504. What man of the Old Testament fed seventy kings under his table?
505. Did God personally investigate the terrible conditions that existed in Sodom and Gomorrah?
506. Did God, man, or Satan ask the first question?
507. What two court officials were hanged for conspiring against their king?
508. The physical beauty of what woman once became a source of danger to her husband ?
509. Is "dementia dollaritis" dangerous to the soul?
510. Which two verses in the Bible contain only two words each?
511. Who was the first Apostle to raise a dead person to life?
512. In what city did a wall fall on twenty-seven thousand men?
513. What color was the only tablecloth mentioned in the Bible?
514. By whom was religious racketeering practiced in the city of Jerusalem?

31

515. What were the children of Israel wearing when they left the land of Egypt?

516. Who was told to drink a little wine for his "stomach's sake"?

517. What is the name of the first mountain mentioned in the Scriptures?

518. Can it be proved that the Apostle Paul had a sister?

519. What did Jesus say concerning "saltless salt"?

520. What people once accused the Lord of hating them?

521. How many letters does the New Testament contain?

522. To whom did Jesus first appear after His resurrection?

523. How many women were aboard Noah's ark during the flood?

524. Who was the only Bible character whose name begins with the letter "Q"?

525. What was the length of "Jacob's ladder"?

526. How did a certain prophet once disguise himself?

527. What was the first thing Noah did when he came out of the ark?

528. Is the title of the once popular song, "Speckled Bird," in the Bible?

529. Who said his belly was ready to burst like new bottles?

530. How many women in the Bible are described as possessing a "good understanding"?

531. Upon what occasion were the Apostles accused of being drunken?

532. Which verse in the Bible contains all the letters of the alphabet except "k"?

533. How many verses does the New Testament contain?

534. Who tore a new garment into twelve pieces while another person was still wearing it?

535. Was cremation ever practiced by the early Jews?

536. How many saints will Jesus bring with Him when He comes again?

537. What man once earned fame as a maker of riddles?

538. Are the Dead Sea and the Mediterranean Sea mentioned by name in the Bible?

539. What noted building was constructed without the sound of hammer or tools being heard?

540. For what price did a horse sell during the days of King Solomon?

541. Did the Jewish women of early Bible times manicure their fingernails?

542. Where is it recorded that by the breath of God, frost is given?

543. What four things are never satisfied?

544. Does the New Testament recommend a specific treatment for the sick?

545. What did manna taste like?

546. Which of the Twelve Apostles was the treasurer?

547. What five-year-old prince was injured because of the carelessness of a nurse?

548. Was there ever a time when everybody spoke the same language?

549. Which of the Old Testament prophets foretold the resurrection of the dead?

550. How many times does the word *sympathy* occur in the Bible?

551. What is the most ancient war on record?

552. Who set up a monument in the middle of a river?

553. What king visited a dying prophet and wept over him?

554. Where is it recorded in the Bible that two sticks became one stick?

555. Of whom was it foretold by an angel that his head should never be shaved?

556. What is the name of the first modern tree mentioned in the Bible?

557. What beloved man of the New Testament paid the hotel bill of a man who had been robbed?

558. Who was the king that was killed by conspirators and brought on horses to his grave?
559. From whom did Moses receive his name, and why?
560. Who used the only penknife mentioned in the Scriptures?
561. What king beat down a city and sowed it with salt?
562. Who was Israel's most wicked king?
563. By whom was the first "temperance society" organized?
564. Which of the Old Testament prophets purchased a field while he was shut up in prison?
565. What well-known prophet instructed a woman to borrow dishes of her neighbor?
566. Is the often-used expression *spare the rod and spoil the child* in the Bible?
567. What color was the manna which the Israelites ate in the wilderness?
568. Whose eyes were said to have "poured out tears"?
569. Which prophet called for music before delivering his prophecy?
570. The king of what city was taken alive in battle and hanged on a tree until dead?
571. What great man wept when those who had injured him asked his forgiveness?
572. Who mortgaged their farms in time of drought to buy corn?
573. How many times did God appear to Solomon?
574. Where in the Scriptures is it recorded that handkerchiefs or aprons were used to heal the sick?
575. Who was first to mention the word *money*?
576. Does the Bible seem to indicate that winking is the sign of an evil mind?
577. Who was forced to drink water that was sprinkled with gold?
578. Whose soul was vexed unto death by his lover?
579. What king of the Old Testament was declared by his people to be worth ten thousand of them?

580. What accident was the occasion of King Ahaziah's death?

581. Whose throat was described as having been dry because of weeping?

582. Who prophesied that the trees of the field shall "clap their hands"?

583. How does a naughty person speak?

584. Was there ever a time when the depths of the sea were frozen?

585. Is it true that the early Jews were commanded to be mindful of and helpful to their neighbor's ass?

586. What kind of wood was used in making ancient musical instruments?

587. Who made a prophecy concerning irrigation?

588. How many famous hunters are mentioned by name in the Bible.

589. For what length of time were the maidens of King Ahasuerus perfumed before they came into his house?

590. What charge did the Prophet Jeremiah bring against certain pastors of his day?

591. Who were the first lobbyists?

592. What two famous brothers were eighty years old before they began their real mission in life?

593. What two men of the Old Testament made golden calves?

594. Who or what in the Bible is referred to as the "washpot" of God?

595. Where in the New Testament is the first recorded sermon preached by the Apostle Paul?

596. How old was David when he died?

597. How many "great women" are mentioned in the Scriptures?

598. Is it true that the Prophet Jeremiah said he once felt like a drunken man?

599. Who was the first woman to wear a bridal vail?

600. Who gave King Solomon an "intelligence test"?

601. What king of Israel loved farming?

602. Can it be proved by both the Old Testament and the New Testament that David was inspired?
603. Who was the Apostle Paul's secretary?
604. By heeding the advice of a little slave-girl, what mighty man of valor was restored to health?
605. How many instances of the dead being raised to life are recorded in the Old Testament?
606. How many men did the Prophet Ezekiel once see worshiping the sun?
607. Who prophesied that the Jews would eat their own children?
608. What well-known man of the Old Testament mentioned the "sins of his youth"?
609. The births of how many distinguished Bible characters were announced by angels?
610. What bird warms her eggs in the dust?
611. What length of time was required by the Egyptians in embalming a dead body?
612. What tree bore twelve different kinds of fruit?
613. Is it true that in olden times certain men could shoot an arrow or throw stones with either hand?
614. Is the expresion *Lord's prayer* in the Bible?
615. What New Testament preacher referred to himself as being "greater than Solomon"?
616. How many people ate at Jezebel's table?
617. Were wagons used as a means of transportation in early Bible times?
618. What is the tenth word of the tenth verse of the tenth chapter of the tenth book of the Bible?
619. What was the first question that God asked man?
620. What man of the Old Testament had thirty sons who rode on thirty asses, and had thirty cities?
621. Since the beginning of Christianity, how many different Jews have claimed to be the promised Messiah?

622. Where in the Bible is it recorded that the faces of certain people were harder than a rock?

623. Who found a swarm of bees and honey in the carcass of a lion?

624. What prominent Old Testament king had eighteen wives and sixty concubines?

625. Was Samson's hair cut off by Delilah, his lover?

626. Where in the Scriptures is it said that a word fitly spoken is like apples of gold in pictures of silver?

627. Are such familiar words as chains, hoods, mufflers, rings, pins, and round tires mentioned in the Bible?

628. Is it true that the women in the early Corinthian church were forbidden to speak during certain church services?

629. How many times is the phrase *everlasting punishment* mentioned in the Bible?

630. Which verse in the Bible contains all the letters of the alphabet except "x"?

631. Where in the Scriptures is the world's first *black-out* recorded?

632. When was the "Authorized" or "King James" translation of the Bible first published?

633. How did Samson's wife die?

634. Which king of Israel reigned only one month?

635. Whose wages were changed ten times?

636. Is there any water in hell?

637. What famous orchestra once "played before the Lord"?

638. Does the New Testament give information as to what language Jesus spoke?

639. Is the expression "brought up" used for "reared" in the Scriptures?

640. What prominent man did God bury in the land of Moab?

641. The motto on United States coins is borrowed from what verse in the Bible?

642. Where in the Bible is there an allusion to the so-called five facts of science, namely: time, space, matter, force, and motion?

643. What Bible once sold for three hundred and seventy-five thousand dollars?

644. What man of the Old Testament slew six hundred Philistines with an ox-goad?

645. Are the words *deity* and *divinity* in the Bible?

646. What three well-known men of the New Testament were partners in the fishing business?

647. Who once thought the Apostle Paul and his co-laborer, Barnabas, were heathen gods?

648. What was the first thing a certain child did after it was raised from the dead?

649. Is there a recorded instance in the Bible of dry bones coming to life?

650. In what unusual place was tax-money once found.

651. Which Old Testament king was quarantined for life because of leprosy?

652. Does the turtle have a voice?

653. What was Joshua's other name?

654. What woman cried, "treason, treason," as she was condemned to die?

655. Are there quotations from every book of the Old Testament in the New Testament?

656. What unusual request did Lot make of two angels before spending the night with him?

657. How many times did Jesus admit His divinity privately?

658. What was the "Vinegar" Bible?

659. What was the first Bible in which italics were used to indicate words which are not in the original?

660. What four men were said to have been less wise than Solomon?

661. When did four vegetarians win a young men's beauty contest?

662. Were the early Jews forbidden to eat blood?

663. What are the teeth of human beings called in the Bible?

664. When did the message of an angel cause a multitude of people to weep?

665. How many reasons did Jesus give for securing a divorce and permitting remarriage?

666. What does the Bible have to say concerning "Gabriel's Horn"?

667. Is it true that the eating of too much honey will produce vomiting?

668. Is the word *Sunday* in the Bible?

669. What famous governor of Judah served twelve years without salary?

670. What is the Bible verse inscribed on the famous Liberty Bell in Independence Hall, Philadelphia?

671. How does the mother eagle carry her young?

672. What popular man of the Old Testament had drinking vessels of gold?

673. Who said that some sins are greater than others?

674. Will there be different degrees of punishment in hell?

675. When was Jesus born?

676. Did God ever authorize soil conservation measures in early Bible times?

677. If the books of Bible were arranged in alphabetical order, which would come first?

678. Who became so excited and frightened that his hair "stood up"?

679. Who owned the only sundial mentioned in the Bible?

680. Who preferred to "abide in the street all night" rather than partake of the hospitality of a great man?

681. What woman of the Old Testament held court under a palm tree?

682. How many books of the Bible have only one chapter each?

683. Who is the only man described in the Scriptures as having been buried in a coffin?

684. What man of the Old Testament stole money from his mother?

685. Is the expression *let your conscience be your guide* in the Bible?

686. In what New Testament city did Christians burn up books worth thousands of dollars?

687. What was the longest period of time that clothing was worn continuously without wearing out?

688. When did the early Jews usually name their children?

689. What well-known man of the Old Testament set fire to three hundred foxes' tails?

690. Whom did the Lord help in battle with hailstones which slew more than the sword?

691. Does the expression, "he is so thin you can count his ribs," have its equivalent in the Bible?

692. From the standpoint of earthly goods, how poor was Christ while He was on earth?

693. How many times is the "screech owl" mentioned in the Bible?

694. What are young widows usually prone to do?

695. Is it true that the children of Judah committed evil deeds about which the Lord had not even thought?

696. What beloved man of the Old Testament died in the nude?

697. Where is it recorded in the Scriptures that against the children of Israel, a dog would not move its tongue?

698. What three noted Bible characters each fasted for forty days?

699. Who said the Apostle Paul's writings were weighty and powerful, but that his speech was contemptible?

700. The deaths of how many of the Twelve Apostles are recorded in the New Testament?

701. Whose heart once became hot?

702. Is the word *church* in the Old Testament?

703. Who was first to write a letter?

704. Where does the Bible allude to the Jewish custom of rubbing new-born infants with salt?

705. Is the following command in the Scriptures: "Be temperate in all things"?

706. What Bible city had the shortest name?

707. Where in the New Testament is it stated that if all Jesus did were written, the world itself could not contain all the books?

708. What colored man led an army of one million men?

709. Where is the account of an iron gate opening of its own accord?

710. What man of the Old Testament was betrayed by the offer of a kiss?

711. Are the words *holy of holies* a Bible phrase?

712. What man found a kingdom while looking for some lost donkeys?

713. What was Esther's Persian or Babylonian name?

714. How many times was the Apostle Paul flogged by the Jews?

715. Who taught the only school mentioned in the Scriptures?

716. What Old Testament prophet gave a description of the ancient method of setting a fractured arm?

717. How many of Adam and Eve's children are mentioned by name?

718. What great man was once food administrator of Egypt?

719. What group of men suffered the humiliation of having their beards partly cut off?

720. Who was King Solomon's mother?

721. The people of what city were always glad to hear of something new?

722. Who was the first singing teacher?

723. The names of what two Bible characters cannot be pronounced without saying "Try"?

724. Where in the Scriptures is a righteous man compared to a tree?

725. What treasurer of New Testament times hanged himself?

726. Who was said to have "died in his own sin"?

727. What does the Bible say about "joining the church"?

728. What is generally considered to be the most beautiful one-sentence prayer ever uttered?

729. What Old Testament prophet had a vision in which he was lifted by a lock of his own hair and carried to the city of Jerusalem?

730. Which word occurs more often in the Scriptures, father or mother?

731. What Old Testament warrior killed eight hundred people with his spear?

732. Whose daughters were called the "fairest in all the land"?

733. Can it be proved that the Apostle Peter was a married man?

734. What woman's advice was sought by five men?

735. Who thought Jesus was John the Baptist raised from the dead?

736. What kind of men did King Saul draft for his army?

737. The occupations of how many of the Tewelve Apostles are revealed in the Bible?

738. Are there more men's or women's names in the Bible?

739. How many idolatrous worshipers of Aaron's golden calf suffered death?

740. What rich man was a secret disciple of Jesus?

741. Who was the first persecutor of Christ?

742. According to the New Testament record, what was the largest number of people converted at any one time?

743. What people had great difficulty in pronouncing the letter "h"?

744. What was the cause of Job's death?

745. What three Old Testament heroes each killed a lion?

746. How was a preacher's room furnished in Old Testament times?

747. What famous boat went aground on a mountain top?

748. What noted man is mentioned by name in connection with the first record of horse-trading in the Bible?

749. Which is mentioned oftener in the Scriptures, the dove or the lion?

750. Where was an altar erected to the "unknown God"?
751. How many soldiers guarded the Apostle Paul while he was a prisoner in Rome?
752. Who was the first efficiency expert?
753. Did King David have brothers?
754. Where is the longest recorded prayer in the New Testament?
755. How many camels did Job own?
756. Who was the first woman to wear an apron?
757. When Moses killed a certain Egyptian, where did he hide the body?
758. What famous New Testament preacher called his hearers "vipers"?
759. How long was darkness over the land while Jesus was on the cross?
760. What military man of the Old Testament had the title of General?
761. Who were accused of "turning the world upside down"?
762. Where in the Scriptures is the statement that "two are better than one"?
763. In what language was the Old Testament originally written?
764. Is it possible for a Gentile to become a Jew?
765. Who was drafted to carry the cross of Jesus to the place of crucifixion?
766. Who saved the Prophet Jeremiah from death in a deep dungeon?
767. Is it recorded in the Scriptures that Jesus sang?
768. What well-known man of the Old Testament hid ear rings under an oak?
769. Do the words *Holy Ghost* occur in the Old Testament?
770. What was the occupation of the Apostle Paul?
771. Did Jesus know He would be crucified in the city of Jerusalem?
772. Who was the first Bible character described as having been buried in a family burying ground?

773. Did Jesus encourage spiritual surgery?
774. What Old Testament king died at sunset?
775. What two babies were born while their mothers were dying?
776. Who was referred to as a "friend of God" three different times?
777. What is the only intoxicating drink specifically mentioned in the Scriptures?
778. Did any one record what Jesus said when He was speaking?
779. Were the feet of Jesus nailed to the cross?
780. Is Nazareth, the childhood home of Jesus, mentioned in the Old Testament?
781. What did the Apostle Paul say is the root of all evil?
782. How many angels are mentioned by name in the Bible?
783. What do the Scriptures have to say concerning the "wandering Jew"?
784. Does the Bible mention major and minor prophets?
785. Do the Jews have an English Version of the Bible?
786. In what way were David and Jonathan related?
787. Upon how many different occasions is Jesus described as weeping?
788. Are the Scriptures silent as to the time and place of the death of Mary, the mother of Jesus?
789. What is the only kind of timepiece mentioned in the Bible?
790. Was Jesus crucified on Mount Calvary?
791. Is the word *sanhedrin* in the Bible?
792. Where in the New Testament is it recorded that Jesus commanded the Apostles to buy swords?
793. Who were told to be content with their wages?
794. How many days were required in rebuilding the walls of Jerusalem?
795. Does the Bible give information as to the kind of wood Jesus' cross was made of?

796. Where in the Scriptures is the expression, "Let the dead bury their dead"?

797. What portions of the Bible have been more widely circulated than others?

798. What was the name of Pilate's wife?

799. What man, after he had sinned, requested the prayers of a righteous man?

800. How many times does the word *Lucifer* occur in the Scriptures?

801. Was Salome the name of Herodias' daughter?

802. What was the age of Jesus at the time of His baptism?

803. In what language was the New Testament originally written?

804. Was the Lord ever described as a "man of war"?

805. Can it be proved that there were three wise men who came from the East to pay homage to the Christ-child?

806. Who was the first man to shear his sheep?

807. Do the Scriptures speak of "good manners"?

808. How many times is Jesus referred to as the "Prince of Peace"?

809. What woman once translated the Bible into the English language?

810. How many prophetesses are mentioned by name in the Bible?

811. Is it predicted by any inspired writer that the human family will become "weaker and wiser"?

812. What were the names of the two thieves who were crucified with Jesus?

813. What chapter in the Bible is known as the "faith chapter"?

814. Who entertained about thirty people in a parlor?

815. Where in the Scriptures is the expression, "holier than thou"?

816. Is the selling of a dog divinely forbidden as some people suppose?

817. How old was Abraham when he was circumcised?

818. Where is the earliest record of God speaking to a king in a dream?

819. What two beloved Bible characters never died?
820. Where is the information that Jesus ate broiled fish and honey?
821. Is it true that Christians are admonished to provoke each other?
822. Where is the divine command to "beware of dogs"?
823. What boy once heard the voice of God?
824. Whose son was healed at one o'clock in the afternoon?
825. What was the name of the nurse who was buried under an oak?
826. Who fell in love at "first sight" at a well?
827. Where is the safest place to keep one's treasures?
828. When was consuming fire quenched in answer to prayer?
829. Who is like a man that takes a dog by the ears?
830. What kind of hands does God hate?
831. Whose tongue was tied until his son was named?
832. What Gentile king assisted in building Solomon's temple?
833. Which Old Testament king was probably the first "henpecked" husband?
834. What man gained fame and also got his name changed by wrestling with an angel?
835. Does the word *Pentateuch* occur in the Bible?
836. What great man of the Old Testament prayed one prayer that was never answered?
837. Who sold his best friend for thirty pieces of silver?
838. What man of the New Testament may easily be identified with a crowing rooster?
839. Where in the Scriptures is it recorded that there is a time to dance?
840. Who was described by the epithet, "that wicked woman"?
841. What well-known man of the Old Testament loved one of his sons more than all his other children?
842. What kind of cloth should be used in patching old garments?
843. For how long should a marriage last?
844. What man of the Old Testament was known as the "grass eating" king?

845. Is the expression *God helps those who help themselves* in the Bible?

846. What kind of musical instrument will be used to wake up the dead?

847. What is the best light for the feet?

848. Where is the world's oldest cemetery?

849. What great man of the Old Testament sought for a witch to call up a dead man?

850. What river is mentioned as being in heaven?

851. Who was his mother's favorite son?

852. Where does the Bible refer to a "builder's estimate"?

853. Who hesitated to speak his opinion because of his youth?

854. Which Old Testament prophet walked naked and barefoot three years "for a sign and wonder"?

855. Who was the only physician mentioned by name in the Scriptures?

856. What part of a ship is used to define Christian hope?

857. Who was the first cave-dweller?

858. How many times does the word *hallelujah* occur in the Bible?

859. Who criticized Christ's "pay envelope"?

860. What man of the Old Testament had seventy of his brothers slain upon one stone?

861. Will hell ever become full?

862. What famous woman was a judge, general, prophetess, and singer?

863. A life without love (charity) is like what kind of musical instrument?

864. What man of the Old Testament was a gatherer of sycamore fruit?

865. Who was the first to have "in-law" trouble?

866. What woman gave David a present of one hundred bunches of raisins?

867. Is the expression *charity begins at home* in the Bible?

868. Where is the recorded instance of one of the most vicious, brutal mutilations in all history?

869. Who won his wife. as a reward for taking a city ?

870. What man of the Old Testament was a terror to himself and to all his friends?

871. Did the people of early Bible times have iron bedsteads?

872. What king was noted for his reckless driving?

873. How many times was the Prophet Jeremiah accused of lying?

874. Who is described in the Bible as being "old and heavy"?

875. What Old Testament king had diseased feet in his old age.?

876. What is the one thing that God cannot do?

877. How many times does the word *philosophy* occur in the Scriptures?

878. Who was the only woman mentioned in the Bible as having been leprous?

879. In what unusual way was Moses' mother related to him?

880. What queen was deposed by her drunken husband because she refused to expose herself?

881. What woman of the New Testament was a tentmaker by trade?

882. Is the expression *everything that glitters is not gold* in the Scriptures?

883. What inspired man hastily accused all men of being liars?

884. What man was described as being "unstable as water"?

885. Which is the longest chapter in the Pentateuch?

886. Who used a boat for both a pulpit and a bed?

887. What part of a ship is used to describe the human tongue?

888. Is the book of Hezekiah in the Old or the New Testament?

889. What became of the garments of Jesus when He was crucified?

890. What did David say about his cup?

891. What kind of ears do some people have?

892. What man started himself on the road to success by his skillful use of a sling?

893. According to Jesus, how many different kinds of builders are there?

894. In early Bible times, what disease did a white hair on a bright spot on the skin indicate?

895. Is a Christian widow permitted to marry any man of her choice?

896. Which of the Twelve Apostles was the first to be killed?

897. What woman murdered a great man with a hammer and nail?

898. Who was the father of eighty-eight children?

899. What king was so unpopular with his people that he "died without being desired"?

900. Who was the world's oldest man?

901. Who had his half-brother killed for insulting his sister?

902. What Old Testament king was murdered while he was "drinking himself drunk"?

903. Who was the first woman to swear?

904. What evil woman forged her husband's name to important letters?

905. What great prophet once said, "my bowels are troubled"?

906. Which king of the Old Testament was murdered by his two sons in a temple?

907. Is the word *Christmas* in the Bible?

908. At one time, what was the combined numerical strength of the armies of Israel and Judah?

909. How many groups of the magic number *seven* are found in the book of Revelation?

910. What man of the New Testament was probably called "shorty" by his intimate friends?

911. What two children's grandfather was also their father?

912. Is the expression *fallen from grace* in the Bible?

913. How many times are the words *Jesus Chirst* placed together in the Four Gospels?

914. What two brothers lost their lives because they used "strange fire"?

915. Were blacksmiths plentiful in Israel?

916. What man of the Old Testament was killed by being stabbed in the bowels?

917. Where is the only recorded instance in the Bible of a mother being paid to nurse her own baby?

918. How many of the Twelve Apostles were said to have wept?

919. How many verses in the Four Gospels are the recorded words of Jesus?

920. What young prince was once hidden by his aunt for a period of six years?

921. Who were the only women described in the Bible as kissing each other?

922. Who had a coat without a seam?

923. Are ferry boats mentioned in the Scriptures?

924. Who was slain as the outcome of a king's birthday party?

925. Who pulled out men's hair because they married foreign wives?

926. Who is the only orator mentioned by name in the Bible?

927. What woman of the Old Testament guarded seven corpses of men from birds and beasts?

928. What prominent man accused his son of making him "stink" among the people?

929. Who married two women of the same name?

930. The good intentions of what man cost him his life?

931. Was Job a perfect man?

932. Was it legal for a Jew to "eat his fill of grapes" from his neighbor's vineyard?

933. Who was ready to die after he had seen the Christ-child?

934. What man of the Old Testament was noted for his swiftness of foot?

935. Who was the tallest man in all Israel?

936. What caused the death of King Jehoram?

937. Was the world's first thief a man or a woman?

938. How many times does the word *stomach* occur in the Bible?

939. What religious woman was accused of being drunken while she was praying?

940. Who stood upon the only pulpit mentioned in the Bible?

941. What woman of the New Testament was a seamstress?

942. Who was the first left-handed man mentioned by name in the Bible?

943. Whose five daughters were the first women to demand their property rights?

944. Who was the only man Scripture records as having washed his face?

945. What queen weaned her nephew in the house of Pharaoh?

946. What did the Prophet Jeremiah once wear about his neck?

947. What woman advised her husband to "curse God and die"?

948. Who was the first preacher to become drunken?

949. What great man made a feast the day his son was weaned?

950. Who was the first shepherdness?

951. Who was the most handsome man of Bible times?

952. Is the often-used expression *bread is the staff of life* in the Bible?

953. The soul of what righteous man was described as having been "vexed from day to day"?

954. Whose mother was said to have "borne him with sorrow"?

955. Who was described as being a "smooth" man?

956. What woman lived in the only college mentioned in the Bible?

957. What man of the Old Testament went to bed and "pouted" because he failed to make a real estate deal?

958. Who was the first president mentioned in the Scriptures?

959. Is the book of Samson in the Old or the New Testament?

960. What well-known man of the Old Testament was as strong, physically, at the age of eighty-five as he was at age forty?

961. Who broke his neck by falling off a seat backwards?

962. Who was the only "fat man" mentioned by name in the Bible?

963. Whose wife wept for seven consecutive days?

964. What woman of the Old Testament circumcised her son with a sharp stone instead of a knife?

965. What man was hanged on the gallows he had prepared for another?

966. Who was the Prophet Jeremiah's secretary?

967. What man in olden times was more than ten feet tall?

968. Who was the first musician?

969. What woman was described as "tender-eyed"?

970. Who was the first woman to despise her husband?

971. What wicked woman was killed by being thrown from a window?

972. What two men of the Old Testament were described as having been "hairy"?

973. Who was the only man to whom God ever promised success?

974. What was the name of Lot's wife?

975. Who hanged himself because his advice was not heeded?

976. Who was called an ass as a compliment?

977. Who was the only man of Bible times described as having been "industrious"?

978. Who was the first to be named before birth?

979. Who, in an emergency, served as both barber and tailor?

980. What man of the Old Testament was the father of seventy-one sons?

981. Who deceived his son-in-law by substituting the bride's sister on the wedding night?

982. Who was the first man to shave himself?

983. What statement did Jesus make that is not recorded in the Four Gospels?

984. What famous woman became a mother at the age of ninety?

52

985. Is it true that the book of Matthew contains all the book of Mark?
986. Was there ever a church in Philadelphia?
987. Did David write all the book of Psalms?
988. What man refused to go into battle without the help of a woman?
989. Who once became so excited his knees "smote one against another"?
990. In early Bible times, was leprosy considered an incurable disease?
991. What woman of the New Testament is sometimes referred to as a "scarlet lily"?
992. Who sold his birthright for a mess of beans?
993. The body of which dead king was to be "cast out in the day to the heat, and in the night to the frost"?
994. What city was to be searched with candles?
995. Was crucifixion a common Jewish punishment?
996. Who was So?
997. Does the word *amen* mean *God bles you*?
998. What group of men carried lamps within empty pitchers?
999. Which Old Testament king hewed a yoke of oxen in pieces?
1000. What man was smothered to death by a thick, wet cloth?
1001. Were any of the books of the Bible written by a woman?
1002. Which chapter in the Bible is known as the *resurrection* chapter?
1003. What kind of meat were the Jews forbidden to eat, though they might sell it or give it away?
1004. Who was next to the oldest man mentioned in the Bible?
1005. Of which king do we read that his nails grew like birds' claws?
1006. How many parables of Jesus are recorded in the New Testament?

1007. Which verse in the Bible mentions cucumbers, melons, leeks, and garlic?

1008. What is the Decalogue?

1009. Where in the Bible is it recorded that a disobedient prophet was killed by a lion?

1010. What food is mentioned most often in the Scriptures?

1011. The corpse of what king was fastened to the wall of a city?

1012. Did Jesus write any of the Bible?

1013. Which Apostle admonished two women to agree?

1014. What man was put on a diet for life?

1015. What great man was displeased with the gift of twenty cities?

1016. Who once said, "My punishment is greater than I can bear"?

1017. What insect is said to live in kings' palaces?

1018. What man of the Old Testament was buried with the "burial of an ass"?

1019. Which book in the Bible ends with two verses which are repeated at the beginning of the first chapter in the next book?

1020. Who gave a certain priest a suit of clothes every year?

1021. What Hebrew official had forty sons and thirty nephews?

1022. Who once ran away from home because he was afraid of his brother?

1023. What man killed a lion on a snowy day?

1024. What man was described as having neither father nor mother?

1025. What man asked another, "how old art thou?"

1026. Who hid one hundred prophets in a cave and fed them bread and water?

1027. Is the word *theater* in the Bible?

1028. What man bought a field and a wife in the same transaction?

1029. Was capital punishment ever prescribed for an animal?

1030. Who was the first man to cremate himself?

1031. Which verse in the Bible mentions oaks, poplars, and elms?

1032. Who went to sleep during a church service and fell out of a window?

1033. Where in the Bible is there a description of a money-box?

1034. What is the Hexateuch?

1035. Which Old Testament king was buried in a city named for himself?

1036. What popular man of the Old Testament invented his own musical instruments?

1037. Who wrote down a prophet's words "with ink" in a book?

1038. Which man of the Old Testament was the father of thirty sons and thirty daughters?

1039. Where in the Scriptures were certain shepherds bidden to howl, cry, and wallow in ashes?

1040. Who secretly explored the ruins of a city by night?

1041. How many years were required in the building of Solomon's house?

1042. Was Moses ever referred to as being a king?

1043. Who bound his own hands and feet with another man's girdle

1044. Is it true that God once prepared a worm for a special purpose?

1045. What victorious leader refused to be made king over Israel?

1046. Is it possible to rob God?

1047. Who once said, "It is better for me to die than to live"?

1048. Which is the only verse in the Bible that mentions fish ponds?

1049. What New Testament ruler was described as a fox?

1050. Which of the prophets was clothed with scarlet?

1051. Who was the first fugitive and vagabond?

1052. How many times does the word *Godhead* occur in the Scriptures?

1053. Where is the account of a monument once being used as a dining table?

1054. What is the name of the first place mentioned in the Bible?

1055. Where is the first recorded prophecy?

1056. Where is the first mention of *liquors* in the Scriptures?

1057. Who was the only herdman mentioned by name in the Bible?

1058. Who in speaking of himself said, "such a dead dog as I am"?

1059. What king sent one of his soldiers to the front of the battle line that he might have his widow for a wife?

1060. Who was the first prisoner of war?

1061. Who once came near being killed for eating a little honey?

1062. What man watched a woman's mouth to see if she was praying?

1063. Who was the first to take an oath or affidavit?

1064. What man made a request to be buried beside his father and mother?

1065. What tribe of Israel was specially characterized by sincerity?

1066. Where is the first mention of giving a tenth to God?

1067. Who was said to have done evil in the sight of the Lord when he was only eight years old?

1068. What Old Testament king shut up the temple of God?

1069. Who was the first man to be sold for money?

1070. Who was the founder of the Hebrew (Jewish) nation?

1071. What woman said, "I am weary of my life"?

1072. Who was the first man to be stoned to death?

1073. What two men of Bible times were ordered to take off their shoes?

1074. If the books of the Old Testament were arranged in alphabetical order, which book would come first?

1075. In which verse in the Bible are six different metals mentioned?

1076. Who passed the sentence of death on his own brother?

1077. Who destroyed the brazen serpent which Moses had made?

1078. What is the Bible penalty for fist fighting?

1079. Unto whom was it said, "Set thine house in order; for thou shalt die, and not live"?

1080. Who, though not a king, was said to have acted in a kingly manner?

1081. Who preferred, in time of trouble, to fall into God's hands than into man's?

1082. Next to the book of Psalms, which book in the Bible has the most chapters?
1083. What banished mother threw her child under a bush to die?
1084. Who was the first soothsayer?
1085. Who was the first "good looking" wife?
1086. What temporal ruler issued a decree that all the world should be taxed?
1087. What man of the New Testament is described as a "doctor of the law"?
1088. Which Old Testament king forsook the counsel of old men and consulted with young men who had been his boyhood friends?
1089. Who referred to himself as the "least of the Apostles"?
1090. Which of the Old Testament prophets was fed by birds?
1091. Who was the only evangelist mentioned by name in the New Testament?
1092. Upon whom did the Savior perform a miracle by the utterance of one word?
1093. What great man was seen about fifteen hundred years after his death?
1094. Does the Bible say that all things are possible with God?
1095. In what did Moses excel all other men?
1096. Who was the only coppersmith mentioned by name in the Bible?
1097. What is the greatest standard of value in the word of God?
1098. What man was struck dumb for not believing what an angel told him?
1099. When was gold and silver as plentiful as stones in the city of Jerusalem?
1100. What city was destroyed and never again inhabited?
1101. Was water ever sold for money in early Bible times?
1102. Who was the first chamberlain mentioned by name in the Scriptures?

1103. What is it that cannot be quenched with water or drowned with floods?

1104. Can there be found in God's word a promise to the wicked?

1105. What was the early Bible name for a prophet?

1106. To what religious sect did the Apostle Paul belong before he became a follower of Christ?

1107. According to the Jewish law, how long did a person remain unclean after touching a dead body?

1108. Who was described as a "prince and a great man"?

1109. Are angels capable of sinning?

1110. Who was the first nurse mentioned by name in the Scriptures?

1111. How many times does the word *depravity* occur in the Bible?

1112. Who was the first man to wear shoes?

1113. Is it true that no man can see God and live?

1114. Where is it recorded in the Bible that the anger of the Lord was "hot"?

1115. Of what baby was it said that God "loved him"?

1116. The friends of what girl mourned her death four days each year?

1117. How long was Christ on the earth after His resurrection from the dead?

1118. Which is the only one of the Ten Commandments that is not found in some form in the New Testament?

1119. In what city did the Apostle Paul "preach a man to death"?

1120. Who told a lie in order to cover his crime?

1121. Which writer of the New Testament was likely not a Jew?

1122. What was the name of Jacob's only daughter?

1123. On what occasion and for what length of time was there silence in heaven?

1124. What was the length of the dagger with which Ehud killed Eglon, king of Moab?

1125. Why did the Israelites ask for a king?

1126. For how long did the sun stand still at the command of Joshua?

1127. Does the Bible make mention of "wise ladies"?

1128. How many men and women were killed in the fall of the building that was pulled down by Samson?

1129. What men refused to give bread to fainting soldiers?

1130. When did God send rain as a sign of His displeasure against Israel?

1131. What was the special avocation of the Gibeonites?

1132. How did the Israelites sharpen their agricultural implements?

1133. What was the punishment threatened the man who should rebuild Jericho?

1134. Does the name *Jesus* occur in the Old Testament?

1135. What article of clothing was the token of a father's partiality?

1136. How many times is the word *apostasy* mentioned in the Bible?

1137. How old was the person upon whom the first miracle was performed after the ascension of Christ?

1138. How often did David praise the Lord?

1139. What two words were used by David in describing the transient nature of his stay on earth?

1140. Unto what did Job liken old age?

1141. How old was Joseph when he was sold by his brothers?

1142. What is harder to be won than a strong city?

1143. Who died full of days, riches, and honor?

1144. Which of the New Testament churches was neither cold nor hot, spiritually?

1145. How long were the Jews in Babylonian captivity?

1146. What plant was miraculously created and destroyed in less than twenty-four hours?

1147. For how many days did the Prophet Ezekiel sit astonished at the river Chebar?

1148. To what kind of sheep did David liken himself?

1149. What great man was commanded to offer his son as a sacrifice?

1150. How many lords of the land were entertained at the feast of Belshazzar?

1151. What king of the Old Testament was guilty of cruelty to animals?

1152. Who was the queen that "proved King Solomon with hard questions?

1153. Is the popular phrase *tower of Babel* in the Bible?

1154. Who, when about to die, charged his son to "show himself a man"?

1155. How many years were required in the building of Herod's temple?

1156. Where is the only instance in the Scriptures of the marriage of a foreign slave to his master's daughter?

1157. Where are apes mentioned in the Bible?

1158. Was the book of Acts of Apostles written by an Apostle?

1159. What city was in such a deplorable condition that the virgins "hung down their heads" for shame?

1160. Where is mention made of land that produced a hundred-fold in one year?

1161. Why did Jacob love Joseph more than all his other children?

1162. Where do the words northward, southward, eastward, and westward occur in one verse in the Bible?

1163. Does the Bible reveal how old Jesus was when He was crucified?

1164. On what mountain was Solomon's temple built?

1165. What man of the Old Testament had brothers that hated him?

1166. Did the people of early Bible times have cancer?

1167. What mountain was purchased by a certain king of Israel upon which to build a city?

1168. Where in the Scriptures was Jesus proclaimed king of the Jews?

1169. At the destruction of what city were all her great men put in chains?

1170. Where is the shortest song in the Bible?

1171. During the early history of the Jews, what punishment was to be inflicted upon a stubborn son?

1172. Which book in the Bible has the fewest verses?

1173. What departing nation borrowed garments of their enemies?

1174. How long did a Hebrew slave have to serve before being given his freedom?

1175. How many saleswomen are mentioned by name in the Bible?

1176. For what period of time did the children of Israel weep for Moses?

1177. What city's name was changed to the name of the conqueror by the conqueror?

1178. Who was referred to as "this cursed woman"?

1179. In Old Testament times, what was the divinely appointed punishment for blasphemy?

1180. Is the expression *haste makes waste* in the Bible?

1181. Did Jesus ever use severity of action?

1182. What is the most familiar temperance text in the Bible?

1183. What usually precedes destruction in the life of an individual?

1184. Lucifer and Ariel are familiar names in literature. Are they also Bible names?

1185. Bethlehem was the birthplace of Jesus and of what other famous Bible character?

1186. How many of the Twelve Apostles were fishermen?

1187. Who made the first recorded confession to the Lord?

1188. Who prayed day and night in the temple?

1189. Is the word *patriarch* in the Old Testament?

1190. What other nation besides Israel was to be scattered throughout the world?

1191. Is an ox sufficiently intelligent to recognize his owner?

1192. What cave was the hiding place of five kings?

1193. Whose name was changed because of cruelty to a prophet?

1194. Who turned his face to the wall in prayer?

1195. What prophet had understanding in all visions and dreams?

1196. Where was the voice of God first heard by human ears?

1197. Who quoted words from Moses that are not found in the Old Testament?

1198. Where is the first *amen* recorded?

1199. How many times does the word *chaplain* occur in the Scriptures?

1200. What king was buried in his own garden?

1201. Where in the Bible is there a dramatic story of a shipwreck?

1202. Who requested that he be given neither poverty nor riches?

1203. Are the books of the Bible arranged in the order in which they were originally written?

1204. What king was cursed and grossly insulted, and by whom?

1205. Who said to her mother-in-law, "whither thou goest I will go"?

1206. What Old Testament queen left a name synonymous with feminine wickedness?

1207. What husband said to his wife, "Am not I better to thee than ten sons"?

1208. What king lost a thousand chariots in battle?

1209. Which is the only book in the Bible that contains more than one hundred chapters?

1210. What king, in besieging a city, made his own conduct an "example for his soldiers"?

1211. Is it true that the Apostle Paul once lost his temper and called a high official a bad name?

1212. What prophetess dwelt under a palm tree?

1213. Will Gabriel's trumpet announce the end of the world?

1214. Which of the Twelve Apostles once cursed and swore?

1215. To whom did "little David" play on his harp?

1216. How many times are the Ten Commandments recorded in the Bible?
1217. What does a "soft answer" do?
1218. Who once prayed, "God, I thank thee that I am not as other men are"?
1219. Is it good or bad when everybody speaks well of an individual?
1220. How many times does the word *baptistery* occur in the Scriptures?
1221. Where is the story in which trees talk?
1222. Does the Bible say anthing of its own authorship?
1223. How many rounds of ammunition did David take with him when he went into his fight with Goliath?
1224. Did Jesus ever pay taxes?
1225. How many words did the Apostle Peter use in describing the life of Jesus?
1226. What is the wages of sin?
1227. Is it possible for a temptation to be so strong that one is not to be blamed if he yields to it?
1228. Which Bible writer tells most about the ressurrection of the dead?
1229. Was Palestine ever a great world power?
1230. Where in the New Testament is a foot race described?
1231. Does the word *its* occur in the King James translation of the Bible?
1232. Why do so many hospitals bear the name of Saint Luke rather than that of Matthew, Mark, or John?
1233. Is the expression *cleanliness is next to godliness* in the Bible?
1234. Who said, "the laborer is worthy of his hire"?
1235. Does the Bible teach that it "pays" to be generous?
1236. When will the end of the world come?
1237. What was it that David had not seen when he was old?
1238. How did Judas die?

1239. What city was described as having been "no mean city"?

1240. The title of the novel, "Gone With the Wind," is an echo from what verse in the Bible?

1241. May one truthfully say that God has tempted him?

1242. What is it that exalts a nation?

1243. What man of the New Testament washed his hands as a symbol of his professed innocence of the death of Jesus?

1244. How many times does the word *anthem* occur in the Bible?

1245. Do the devils believe in God?

1246. Who once said, "dust thou art and unto dust shalt thou return"?

1247. Who was Moses' father-in-law?

1248. While Jesus was on earth, could the Jews inflict the death penalty?

1249. How many years were required in writing the Bible?

1250. What man of the Old Testament disguised himself in an effort to deceive his father?

1251. How many times does the word *Palestine* occur in the Scriptures?

1252. Which Jewish high priest was said to have been clothed with filthy garments?

1253. Are the words *senators* and *senate* in the Bible?

1254. What woman went to her wedding on a camel?

1255. What famous man of the Old Testament requested that he not to be buried in Egypt?

1256. Which prophet smote another prophet on the cheek?

1257. Who was raised to life after having been in the grave four days?

1258. What man slept with stones for a pillow?

1259. Did the early Jews like hogs?

1260. What boy overheard a plot, and saved the life of the Apostle Paul?

1261. The eyes of what man were not dim when he was one hundred and twenty years old?
1262. What was the scriptural name for clothes of mourning?
1263. Is there any mention of the *cross* in the Old Testament?
1264. What were the last recorded words of Jesus before He ascended to heaven?
1265. Who was tempted on a high mountain?
1266. What three grains are most often mentioned in the Bible?
1267. Where is it recorded that twelve men were baptized twice?
1268. Are lemons and oranges mentioned in the Scriptures?
1269. Who offered "thirty changes of garments" for solving a riddle?
1270. What kind of bird did Noah first send out of the ark?
1271. Which books of the Bible were written by brothers of Jesus?
1272. What woman was referred to as the "mother of all living"?
1273. Do angels marry?
1274. Behind what kind of trees did the troops of David hide?
1275. Which Old Testament king had the longest reign?
1276. Which of the Old Testament prophets is most frequently quoted in the New Testament?
1277. Is there scriptural warrant for the expression, "guardian angel"?
1278. Will there ever be another flood?
1279. Who was Noah's grandfather?
1280. What were the first words Jesus spoke from the cross?
1281. What animal cannot change its spots?
1282. When was the first complete Hebrew Bible printed?
1283. Has God ever sent rain on some, and withheld it from others?
1284. Who was referred to as the "beauty of Israel"?
1285. How far is it between life and death?
1286. Is it possible for one to hide from God?
1287. What is the most wicked and deceitful thing known to man?
1288. How many times does the word *reverend* occur in the Bible?

1289. What man of the New Testament is known today only because of his "good neighbor" policy?

1290. Did the early Jews regard the camel as being good for food?

1291. What woman "fifth columnist" aided the fall of Jericho?

1292. In the New Testament, an unsaved person is compared to what animal?

1293. What was the weight of Goliath's coat?

1294. Has God ever spoken in secret to man?

1295. Who were said to have been swifter than eagles and stronger than lions?

1296. What musical instruments contributed to the fall of a great city?

1297. In the Bible, what is the meaning of the word *birthright*?

1298. What people in early times liked garlic?

1299. Which Apostle's mother-in-law is mentioned in the Bible?

1300. Could the Jews of Old Testament times immediately marry a beautiful woman captured in warfare?

1301. What flower is described as being more beautiful than a certain lavishly dressed king?

1302. What woman agreed with her husband to tell a lie for a profit?

1303. What Biblical town became famous for its poor hotel accommodations on an important occasion?

1304. Was Jesus born in a manger?

1305. Who built the city of Nineveh?

1306. Are quotation marks used in the King James Translation of the Bible?

1307. Were Jesus and John the Baptist related?

1308. Where in the Bible is Jesus referred to as a "man of sorrows"?

1309. Does a spider have hands?

1310. Who was the first convert to Christianity in Europe?

1311. Is *holy water* mentioned in the Scriptures?

1312. What man mourned when his child was sick, but did not mourn after the child had died?

1313. Was Jesus ever referred to as being the son of Joseph?

1314. Which is the longest verse in the Bible?

1315. How many chosen men among the Benjamites were left-handed?

1316. What is the ornament of a Christian woman?

1317. Can it be proved that Jesus ever smiled?

1318. In which chapter of the book of Matthew is there a description of the Last Judgment?

1319. What is promised to those who wait upon the Lord?

1320. Are rats mentioned in the Bible?

1321. How many times is Jesus described as *standing* on the right hand of God?

1322. What four men were smitten under the fifth rib?

1323. How many men of early Bible times lived to be more than nine hundred years old?

1324. How many times does the word *and* occur in the Scriptures?

1325. What king was slain by a prophet?

1326. Which of the Twelve Apostles was a tax collector?

1327. When was the Revised Version of the English Bible first published?

1328. Is it true that the name of Jesus Christ occurs in the first and in the last verse of the New Testament?

1329. What man was referred to as a "half-baked" cake?

1330. Who said, "Be sure your sin will find you out"?

1331. What child's father, mother, grandfather, and uncle died about the same time?

1332. How many different kinds of food are mentioned in the Bible?

1333. What was the name of Abraham's second wife?

1334. Who was stoned to death for theft?

1335. What woman was made barren because she rebuked her husband?

1336. What man of the Old Testament was mocked by an ass?

1337. Who was condemned to death for prophesying falsely?

1338. What is the name of the only street mentioned in the Bible?

1339. What man was once asked if he could speak Greek?

1340. The names of how many Bible persons begin with the letter "V"?

1341. When was the American Revised Version of the English Bible first published?

1342. Can it be proved that Job was a Hebrew, or Jew?

1343. Is the word *Catholic* in the Bible?

1344. Where in the Bible is there something said about a "still small voice"?

1345. What is the name of the first city mentioned in the New Testament?

1346. Which is the middle chapter of the Bible?

1347. Who were the only two women whose ages are recorded in the Scriptures?

1348. What man broke all the Ten Commandments at one time?

1349. Which prophet once mentioned something about boiling bones?

1350. How many different kinds of birds and fowls are mentioned in the Bible?

1351. Is the word *prejudice* in the Scriptures?

1352. The Christian zeal of what great man was attributed to madness?

1353. Who was David's counsellor?

1354. What well-beloved widow once ate parched corn?

1355. Which is the longest chapter in the Bible?

1356. Of whom was it said, "there was no blemish in him"?

1357. Who was the only person who raised a voice in behalf of Jesus during His trials?

1358. Whose life was miraculously restored by the Prophet Elijah?

1359. What man of the Old Testament slew three hundred people with a spear?

1360. What wicked king delayed punishment due him by humbling himself?

1361. Where in the Bible is a legal transfer of real estate described in detail?

1362. Which Old Testament king had a throne of ivory?

1363. Before what mountain were flocks and herds forbidden to graze?

1364. Whose life was endangered by a conspiracy of more than forty people?

1365. Are the expressions *fatherhood of God* and *brotherhood of man* in the Bible?

1366. Who slew himself in order to slay his enemies?

1367. Who disguised themselves by wearing old clothes?

1368. Who was twice aroused from sleep by the touch of an angel?

1369. Upon whom did Moses once bestow a kiss?

1370. What starving man was revived by means of bread, water, figs, and raisins?

1371. How many chapters does the New Testament contain?

1372. Is the word *happiness* in the Bible?

1373. Which prophet described men's faces as turning pale with fear?

1374. What man of the Old Testament was referred to as the "Tishbite"?

1375. Was Esau a bachelor at the time he married two women?

1376. Where in the Scriptures is a lengthy description of a perfect wife?

1377. What man washed his garments in wine?

1378. How many times is the word *mules* mentioned in the New Testament?

1379. Which is the shortest psalm in the book of Psalms?

1380. What man and his wife were buried in a cave?

1381. Can it be proved that Jesus will ever put His feet upon this earth again?

1382. Is there a probable allusion to "sign language" in the Scriptures?

1383. Is Satan described in the Bible as a personality or as a mere influence?

1384. What blind man once kissed his two grandsons?

1385. The son of what harlot judged Israel for six years?

1386. What woman of the Old Testament became a mineral?

1387. Which Apostle was shipwrecked three times?

1388. What people in New Testament times were referred to as "slow bellies"?

1389. Which of the Old Testament prophets foretold an eclipse of the sun?

1390. What preacher was stoned to death for preaching a sermon?

1391. What king, after having made a speech, was immediately "eaten of worms"?

1392. During the early history of the Jews what was the divinely appointed punishment for defiling the Sabbath?

1393. Who, in Old Testament times, shot an arrow through a man's body?

1394. What two sisters were the mothers of their half brothers?

1395. The right ear of what man was amputated with a sword?

1396. How many times does the word *Selah* occur in the book of Psalms?

1397. Which Old Testament king married fourteen wives?

1398. What animal once saw an angel?

1399. What woman, while dying, named her new-born baby?

1400. Who was Cain's wife?

ANSWERS

1. Only one time. Mark 3:5
2. Yes. Judges 13:17,18
3. Yes. Proverbs 30:33
4. To multiply and replenish the earth. Genesis 1:27,28
5. Six hundred and thirteen
6. From aprons of fig leaves to coats of skin. Genesis 3:7,21
7. The longest verse. See Esther 8:9; Psalms 117
8. Fig poultice. 2 Kings 20:5-7; Isaiah 38:21
9. No. Psalms 32:9
10. Eve, Hannah, and Anna. Genesis 3:20; 1 Samuel 2:1; Luke 2:36
11. Yes. Isaiah 7:20
12. Lot. Genesis 19:30-38
13. Noah and Job. Genesis 6:9; Job 1:1,8
14. Yes. Joshua 1:7,8
15. Ahaz. 2 Kings 16:2,20; 2 Kings 18:1,2
16. Death. Exodus 21:16
17. Jezebel. 2 Kings 9:30
18. Yes. Numbers 27:1
19. Song of Solomon
20. 2 Kings 4:38-41
21. No
22. Yes, Hebrews 11:4
23. Four hundred and ninety. Matthew 18:21,22
24. Yes, apparently so. Judges 20:15,16
25. A chariot. 1 Kings 10:29
26. Psalms 103:1 or 2
27. Yes, an Ethiopian. Numbers 12:1
28. Seven thousand. Job 1:1,3
29. Yes. Proverbs 18:24
30. Proverbs 6:16-19
31. Some Bible students think so. Nahum 2:4
32. Yes. Psalms 14:2,3
33. No
34. Yes. Deuteronomy 20:1,2,8
35. Mules. Genesis 36:24
36. Yes. Genesis 5:1,2
37. 773,692
38. Forty-two thousand. Judges 12:5,6
39. 2 Chronicles 20:17
40. Great toe. Judges 1:6,7
41. Yes. Deuteronomy 22:5
42. Acts 21
43. Maachah. 2 Chronicles 11:21
44. Hezekiah. 2 Kings 20:20
45. No
46. 2 Kings 2:19-22
47. No
48. Esther. Esther 2:7
49. David. Psalms 56:1,8
50. Job. Job 1:8
51. No
52. Ananias. Acts 23:1,2
53. The cat
54. 3,566,480
55. The serpent. Genesis 3:14,15
56. Paul. Acts 26:9-11; Galatians 1:13
57. 2 Kings 6:1-7
58. Yes. 1 Corinthians 6:9,10
59. 31,102
60. A moment. 1 Corinthians 15:51,52
61. Yes. Ecclesiastes 5:12
62. "Outlandish." Nehemiah 13:26
63. Jacob. Genesis 35:19,20
64. 2 Kings 6:24-29
65. Abraham and Ishmael. Genesis 17:24-26
66. David. 1 Chronicles 28:2-4
67. Maher-shalal-hash-baz. Isaiah 8:3
68. Salt. Colossians 4:6
69. The "prodigal son." Luke 15:11-16
70. Abraham. Genesis 20:11,12
71. Only one time. Isaiah 57:15
72. Brothers. Genesis 22:20,21
73. Yes. Leviticus 11:7,8
74. Psalms 136
75. Jacob and Rachel. Genesis 29:10,28
76. Solomon. 1 Chronicles 22:7-9
77. The book of conversions.
78. 1250 A. D. by Cardinal Hugo.
79. Job. Job 10:20,21
80. Esther
81. In the Jordan river. Mark 1:9
82. One thousand and seventy-two.
83. 1550 A. D. by Robert Stevens, a printer in Paris, France.
84. 1535 A. D. by Miles Coverdale.

85. For "gadding about." Jeremiah 2:31,36
86. Genesis, fifth chapter.
87. The Latin Bible, 1455 A. D.
88. 1782 A. D.
89. John Wycliffe, 1382 A. D. This translation was from the Latin and was written in longhand.
90. King Josiah. 2 Chronicles 35:20,21
91. 1828 A. D.
92. In the streets. Jeremiah 7:17,18
93. Belteshazzar. Daniel 1:7
94. Yes. 2 Peter 2:22
95. 1865 A. D.
96. Elijah. 2 Kings 2:11
97. Jochebed. Exodus 6:20
98. Daniel. Daniel 6:4-16
99. No
100. Nineveh. Jonah 4:11
101. King Saul. 1 Samuel 20:32-34
102. Yes. Psalms 147:4
103. Balaam. Numbers 22:29
104. Thirty-three hundred and forty.
105. Yes. 1 Chronicles 13:12
106. In the "hinder parts." Psalms 78:65,66
107. David. 1 Samuel 18:27
108. 1816 A. D.
109. Manoah. Judges 13:15,16
110. No
111. Egypt. Genesis 46:34
112. Three years and six months. Luke 4:25
113. Acts 17:17
114. Jesus. Matthew 7:12
115. King Ahasuerus. Esther 1:10-12
116. 1 Chronicles 1:25
117. Three: Matthew 10:2-4; Luke 6:13-16
118. Yes. Mark 6:1-3
119. The Apostles. Mark 16:9-11; Luke 24:1-11
120. Fourteen
121. Sisera. Judges 4:18,19
122. Death. Deuteronomy 22:23,24
123. Psalms 107, verses 8,15,21,31
124. Yes. Jeremiah 48:36-39
125. Eight. 1 Peter 3:18-20
126. Proverbs
127. Genesis 3:20
128. Yes. Ecclesiastes 7:1
129. Jacob. Genesis 29:11,17
130. Boaz. Ruth 4:7-9
131. "My God, my God, why hast forsaken me?" Matthew 27:46
132. Yes. 2 Kings 21:13
133. One hundred shekels. Deuteronomy 22:16-21
134. Son of Zephaniah. Zechariah 6:14
135. The Prophet Elijah. 1 Kings 19:1-4
136. Mount Olivet. Acts 1:12
137. Samuel. 1 Samuel 12:1,2
138. Suddenly. Acts 2:1-4
139. The wicked. Isaiah 48:22
140. Jesus. John 13:3-5
141. Her name is not revealed in the Bible.
142. At the close of each day. Leviticus 19:13; Deuteronomy 24:14,15
143. Proverbs 18:22
144. Isaiah. Isaiah 4:1
145. Rotten rags. Jeremiah 38:7-13
146. Only one time each. Joel 3:3
147. Yes. Amos 2:6
148. No
149. David. 2 Samuel 12:1-7
150. The Prophet Elijah. 1 Kings 18:22,40; 1 Kings 19:1-3
151. Moses. Exodus 4:10
152. Moses and Aaron. Deuteronomy 34:1-5; Numbers 20:28
153. Five: King Saul, King Saul's armor-bearer, Ahithophel, Zimri, and Judas Iscariot. 1 Samuel 31:4; 1 Samuel 31:5; 2 Samuel 17:23; 1 Kings 16:18; Matthew 27:3-5
154. Yes. Revelation 12:7
155. Two hours. Acts 19:24-34
156. Nathanael. John 1:49
157. Jerusalem. Jeremiah 7:29
158. Approximately two hundred and fifty.
159. His linen girdle. Jeremiah 13:1
160. Jabin. Judges 4:2,3

161. Yes. Ecclesiastes 3:1,2
162. Yes. Ecclesiastes 7:17
163. Job. Job 6:6
164. 2 Kings 4:8,16
165. The disobedient. Leviticus 26:14-16
166. The flesh of any wild animal or bird.
167. The Prophet Jeremiah. Jeremiah 51:60-63
168. Yes. Exodus 32:14
169. Yes. Leviticus 11:6,29
170. 1901 A. D.
171. Jedidiah. 2 Samuel 12:24,25
172. The tongue. James 3:7,8
173. No. Job 32:9
174. Paul and Barnabas. Acts 15:36-40
175. Because they give an outline or synopsis of Christ's life.
176. Isaiah. Isaiah 28:20
177. Yes. Leviticus 11:20
178. Ahab. 1 Kings 22:39
179. Yes, once. Amos 8:9; Matthew 27:45
180. As fools. Psalms 14:1
181. Achan. Joshua 7:20,21
182. Yes. Acts 17:30
183. Seven. 1 Kings 6:37,38
184. Yes. 1 Samuel 26:20
185. Only one time. Numbers 11:5
186. The Zebulunites. Judges 5:14
187. Yes. 1 Corinthians 11:14
188. Ezekiel 44:17,18
189. Amos. Amos 5:19
190. Four: Numbers 7. 1 Chronicles 6. Psalms 119. Luke 1
191. 1812 A. D.
192. King Saul. 1 Samuel 31:4-6
193. 2 Thessalonians
194. Job
195. King Pharaoh. 1 Kings 9:16
196. Old women. Titus 2:3
197. Only new translations may be copyrighted.
198. Yes. Exodus 35:3
199. Only once. Proverbs 14:14
200. Samuel. 1 Samuel 7:15-17
201. One thousand and five songs,

and three thousand proverbs. 1 Kings 4:30,32
202. Yes. Leviticus 2:7; Leviticus 7:9
203. Ahasuerus, Nebuchadnezzar, and Darius. Esther 6:1; Daniel 2:1; Daniel 6:9,18
204. Only one time. Luke 15:25
205. Hosea. Hosea 4:16
206. Yes. Numbers 31:3-6; Numbers 1:1-3
207. Absalom. 2 Samuel 18:18
208. Yes. Luke 4:14-16; John 8:6
209. Isaiah 44:9-17
210. The Gadites. 1 Chronicles 12:8
211. 2 Kings 19 and Isaiah 37
212. Ben-haded. 2 Kings 6:24-32
213. Jeroboam. 1 Kings 13:4
214. Jonah. Jonah 3:4,10; Jonah 4:1-5
215. The conduct of the people of Jerusalem. Ezekiel 16:43
216. Ezekiel. Ezekiel 7:17
217. Only one time. Acts 12:4
218. Three. Daniel 3:20,21
219. Samson. Judges 14:12-18
220. Yes. Ezekiel 27:24
221. Ten. Esther 9:12-14
222. Peter. Luke 5:8
223. Yes. Psalms 44:23
224. No
225. On the same day of the execution. Deuteronomy 21:22,23
226. The Prophet Jeremiah. Jeremiah 9:1
227. One hundred and fifty-three. John 21:11
228. Israel. Jeremiah 3:6-8
229. Og and Saul. Deuteronomy 3:11; 1 Samuel 10:21-23
230. "Nothing." Job 26:7
231. Ahasuerus. Esther 1:2-4
232. Two hundred and eighty-eight. 1 Chronicles 25:5-7
233. Thirty-three. 1 Kings 20:16
234. Elisha. 1 Kings 19:19-21
235. David. 2 Samuel 23:15-17
236. No
237. Job. Job 1:13-22
238. Yes. Genesis 50:2
239. Seventy. Judges 1:7

240. Numbers 15:32-36
241. Yes. James 3:7
242. The feeding of the five thousand. Matthew 14:15-21; Mark 6:35-44; Luke 9:12-17; John 6:5-14
243. Luke
244. Obadiah
245. Every day. Psalms 7:11
246. Jeremiah. Jeremiah 17:1
247. Peter. Matthew 16:23
248. Job. Job 34:36,37
249. Only one time. Luke 23:33
250. Jericho. Deuteronomy 34:3
251. Asa. 2 Chronicles 15:16
252. Noah, Daniel, and Job. Ezekiel 14:14
253. Yes. Third John 1:13
254. Yes. Ecclesiastes 7:8
255. David. 1 Samuel 21:12-15
256. Proverbs 30:25
257. A storm, a fire, and an earthquake. 1 Kings 19:8-12
258. Yes. Exodus 8:2,3
259. Only one time. Zechariah 2:12
260. Abraham. Genesis 12:14-20
261. Jeremiah. Jeremiah 4:19
262. Yes, half-brothers. Matthew 13:53-55
263. Yes. Mark 6:3
264. Job. Job 19:17
265. Ahab. 1 Kings 16:33
266. Jesus. Luke 10:17,18
267. Five. Matthew 14:15-21
268. The Cretians. Titus 1:12,13
269. Yes. Romans 16:16
270. Cain. Genesis 4:17
271. They cut down all the trees and filled up the wells. 2 Kings 3:21-25
272. Yes. Luke 19:23
273. Mules, horses, camels, and young dromedaries. Esther 8:7-10
274. James. James 2:1-4
275. Sixteen. Hebrews 11:4-33
276. Yes. Ezekiel 8:7-10
277. Satan. 1 Chronicles 21:1
278. Job and Jeremiah. Job 3:1-11; Jeremiah 20:14,15
279. No
280. Hemorrhoids. 1 Samuel 5:6,9
281. Malachi 4:5,6
282. 1 Samuel 9:2
283. Yes apparently so. 1 Kings 4:30-34
284. David. Psalms 22:14
285. About six pounds. 2 Samuel 14:25,26
286. Two or three. Deuteronomy 19:15
287. Derbe. Acts 14:20
288. Two Genesis 50:2,26
289. Yes. Deuteronomy 22:10
290. Baskets. 2 Kings 10:1,6,7
291. Yes. 2 Kings 17:31
292. The Syrian army. 2 Kings 7:3-7
293. Mount Gilboa. 2 Samuel 1:5-12
294. Six hundred shekels of gold. 1 Chronicles 21:18-25
295. Noah. Genesis 6:14-22
296. Nazareth. John 1:46
297. His mantle. 2 Kings 2:11-15
298. Four thousand. 2 Chronicles 9:25
299. Yes. Joshua 24:12
300. Three: Joshua 3:14-17; 2 Kings 2:6-8; 2 Kings 2:12-14
301. The Sidonians. 1 Kings 5:6
302. No
303. Job 28
304. One. 2 Kings 4:18-20
305. One hnudred and forty years. Job 42:16
306. It was first printed in 1550 A. D. and was compiled by John Marbeck.
307. Three. Song of Solomon 8:6
308. Four: 1 Kings 13:23-32; 1 Kings 20:35,36; 2 Kings 2:23,24; Daniel 6:24
309. No. Leviticus 21:1,14
310. In a hole of the rock near the river Euphrates. Jeremiah 13:1-5
311. The first nine words of Psalms 22:1
312. The sons of King Saul. 2 Samuel 21:1-9
313. Yes, apparently so. Isaiah 11:12; Revelation 7:1
314. 1 Chronicles 5:18-21
315. 2 Corinthians 13:14

76

316. One thousand eight hundred and forty.
317. Psalms 117
318. Yes, published in 1883 A. D.
319. Less than five.
320. No. Deuteronomy 24:5
321. Three: Matthew 14:15-21; Matthew 15:32-38; John 2:7-11
322. Jonah. Jonah 1:3
323. Ezra 10:9,13
324. Pharaoh's chief baker. Genesis 40:20-22
325. The Chaldeans. Habakkuk 1:6-8
326. Yes. 1 Kings 15:22
327. Herod's. Acts 12:21,22
328. The ant, coney, locust, and spider. Proverbs 30:24-28
329. Lot's wife. Luke 17:32
330. They lost their hands and feet and were hanged. 2 Samuel 4:5-12
331. Michal. 1 Samuel 19:11-16
332. Yes, apparently so. 1 Corinthians 5:9
333. No
334. Yes, especially in cold weather. Ecclesiastes 4:11
335. Yes. 2 Samuel 20:9
336. Zechariah 12:4
337. Mustard. Matthew 13:31,32
338. David's
339. After the death of the person who made it. Hebrews 9:16,17
340. Joshua. Joshua 24:22
341. Selehammahlekoth. 1 Samuel 23:28
342. Second John
343. 1471 A. D.
344. Yes. Exodus 30:22-28
345. Isaiah. Isaiah 19:1
346. Acts 27:14-28
347. Adam, nine hundred and thirty years. Genesis 5:5
348. Aaron. Leviticus 16:3,4
349. Yes. 2 Kings 4:32-37
350. Revelation 16:21
351. Abraham. Genesis 14:13
352. Joseph. Genesis 37:28
353. Isaiah. Isaiah 49:23

354. Damascus. Genesis 14:15
355. Ben-hadad. 2 Kings 8:7-15
356. Yes. 2 Kings 10:18-25
357. Jeremiah 28:15-17
358. 1947 A. D.
359. Jewish women. Isaiah 3:17,24
360. Zaccheus. Luke 19:1-4
361. Daniel. Daniel 7:28
362. Rebekah. Genesis 27:15,16
363. Five hundred. 2 Chronicles 13:17
364. Forty days. 1 Kings 19:1-8
365. Read Luke 4:16-29
366. Yes. Malachi 4:6; Revelation 22:21
367. Gideon and Ornan. Judges 6:11; 1 Chronicles 21:20
368. Isaiah 29:8
369. Approximately ninety times.
370. Matthew, Mark, Luke, and John.
371. Yes. John 4:9
372. Pharaoh. Jeremiah 46:17
373. John 11:35
374. Yes. Jeremiah 6:8,15
375. 1663 A. D. by John Eliot.
376. New Hampshire
377. The Apostle Peter. 1 Peter 3:7
378. Yes. Job 19:20
379. Seven hundred wives and three hundred concubines. 1 Kings 11:1,3
380. About thirty-two thousand.
381. Job. Job 19:23
382. Yes. Job 39:25
383. 1 Kings 3:16-19
384. Yes. Acts 17:26
385. Jonah. Jonah 2:1
386. Daniel 4:37
387. Taverner's Great Bible, published in 1539 A. D. and was so called because of its size and the fact it was chained in the churches so it could not be carried away.
388. John 3:16
389. Many Bible students think so. Job 38:35
390. Cain. Genesis 4:17
391. Yes. Psalms 78:25
392. Isaiah. Isaiah 40:22
393. Israel. Jeremiah 51:19,20

394. Genesis 1:3
395. Fifty thousand and seventy. 1 Samuel 6:19
396. Yes. Leviticus 19:28
397. No
398. Ezra 7:21
399. Ninety feet. Daniel 3:1
400. No. All of Cain's descendants were destroyed in the flood. Noah descended from Seth, not from Cain. Genesis 5:3-32. Noah and his family were saved in the ark. 1 Peter 3:20. All the others were lost in the flood waters. Therefore, Cain has no descendants this side of the flood.
401. "In the way he should go." Proverbs 22:6
402. Aaron. Exodus 17:8-13
403. Samuel's. 1 Samuel 8:1-3
404. Rebekah. Genesis 25:21-28
405. Job. Job 10:10
406. Satan. Job 2:4
407. Ten. Genesis 18:32; Genesis 19:24
408. A certain giant. 2 Samuel 21:20
409. Twice. Matthew 8:5-10, Mark 6:1-6
410. Solomon. Ecclesiastes 9:4
411. Elijah. 1 Kings 18:20-40
412. More than forty. Acts 23:12-14
413. No
414. Yes, he was not afraid of ten thousand people. Psalms 3:6
415. Yes, once. Hebrews 3:1
416. Elisha. 1 Kings 19:19
417. Deuteronomy 23:18
418. Yes, the Apostle Paul. 1 Timothy 5:8
419. Isaiah. Isaiah 19:4-7
420. The Prophet Jeremiah. Jeremiah 15:18
421. Yes. Proverbs 17:28
422. More than three feet. Numbers 11:31
423. Yes. Luke 2:41-51
424. One time. Numbers 14:34
425. They mortgaged their homes and their land. Nehemiah 5:3,4

426. Fifteen. 2 Kings 20:1-6
427. 1 Kings, chapter eight.
428. Absalom. 2 Samuel 18:9
429. James and John. Mark 3:17
430. Yes. 1 Kings 15:5
431. Simeon and Levi. Genesis 34:1-27
432. Only one time. 2 Samuel 23:1
433. Yes. Exodus 22:25
434. They were employed both day and night. 1 Chronicles 9:33
435. "The house appointed for all living." Job 30:23
436. Four: Genesis 3:20; Genesis 4:19,22
437. Yes. Revelation 1:8
438. Paul. Acts 28:30
439. Some Bible students think so. 2 Peter 3:10-12
440. This word is not in the Bible.
441. No accounts were kept. 2 Kings 22:3-7
442. Nothing
443. Yes. Acts 7:45; Colossians 4:11
444. Twice: 1 Samuel 12:16-18; James 5:17,18
445. Joseph. Genesis 37:17-19
446. A crippled man. Acts 3:1-10
447. A person is a sinner because he sins.
448. David. Psalms 109:23
449. First Thessalonians
450. Yes. Exodus 22:1-3
451. Jeremiah. Jeremiah 8:7
452. Yes. Revelation 9:6
453. Fourteen: David, Abraham, and and the twelve sons of Jacob, Acts 2:29; Hebrews 7:4; Acts 7:8
454. Three thousand nine hundred and twenty.
455. No
456. Yes. Proverbs 30:5,6; Revelation 22:18
457. The lion. Proverbs 30:30
458. To "die the death of the righteous." Numbers 23:5,10
459. Isaac. Genesis 24:63
460. This expression is not in the Scriptures.

461. 1 Kings 9:26-28
462. Samson's, Absalom's, and the sinful woman's. Judges 16:13-17; 2 Samuel 14:25,26: Luke 7:36-47
463. Approximately ten.
464. David. 2 Samuel 20:3
465. Eighty pieces of silver. 2 Kings 6:25
466. The Lord. Genesis 18:13,14
467. Revelation 20:4
468. See Luke 2:49
469. No. John 10:41
470. In Samaria "in the corner of a bed." Amos 3:12
471. Yes. Matthew 26:55,56
472. The proud. Psalms 119:69,70
473. John the Baptist. Matthew 3:1-4
474. Pharaoh. Genesis 41:42
475. Heavier than the sands of the sea. Job 6:1-3
476. Ten thousand six hundred and eighty-four.
477. The dove
478. Zedekiah. 2 Kings 25:7
479. Dukes. Genesis 36:15-16
480. Zimri. 1 Kings 16:15
481. Felix, Festus, and Fortunatus. Acts 23:24; Acts 25:1; 1 Corinthians 16:17
482. Saul. 1 Samuel 26:21
483. A eunuch of Ethiopia. Acts 8:26-39
484. Only one time. Matthew 27:46
485. No
486. See Exodus 32:19,20
487. By a river. Genesis 2:10
488. Adam. Genesis 2:19
489. Shallum's. Nehemiah 3:12
490. The Apostle Peter. 2 Peter 3:15,16
491. Egypt. Jeremiah 46:20
492. Genesis 29:15-20
493. Gideon. Judges 6:11-19
494. Jacob and Esau. Genesis 25:24-28
495. Pharaoh. Exodus 8:1-8
496. Cain. Genesis 4:8
497. They sat silently by his side for seven days and seven nights. Job 2:11-13

498. That of Jonathan and David. 1 Samuel 18:1-4
499. Saul. 1 Samuel 18:8,9
500. Yes, probably so. Isaiah 60:8
501. Adullum. 1 Samuel 22:1,2
502. Jonathan and Ahimaaz. 2 Samuel 17:17-19
503. No
504. Adonibezek. Judges 1:7
505. Yes. Genesis 18:20,21
506. Satan. Genesis 3:1
507. Bigthan and Teresh. Esther 2:21-23
508. Rebekah. Genesis 26:6-11
509. Yes. 1 Timothy 6:10
510. John 11:35; 1 Thessalonians 5:16
511. Peter. Acts 9:40
512. Aphek. 1 Kings 20:30
513. Blue. Numbers 4:7
514. Jewish priests. John 2:13-16
515. Harness. Exodus 13:18
516. Timothy. 1 Timothy 1:1,2; 1 Timothy 5:23
517. Ararat. Genesis 8:4
518. Yes. Acts 23:16
519. He said it is of no value. Matthew 5:13
520. The Israelites. Deuteronomy 1:27
521. 838,380
522. A woman. Mark 16:9
523. Four. Genesis 7:13
524. Quartus. Romans 16:23
525. It reached from earth to heaven. Genesis 28:10-12
526. By putting ashes on his face. 1 Kings 20:38
527. He built an altar unto the Lord. Genesis 8:15-20
528. Yes. Jeremiah 12:9
529. Elihu. Job 32:6,19
530. Only one. 1 Samuel 25:3
531. On the day of Pentecost, but Peter proved they were sober. Acts 2:1-21
532. Galatians 1:14
533. Seven thousand nine hundred and fifty-nine.
534. Ahijah. 1 Kings 11:29,30
535. No

536. Ten thousands. Jude 1:14
537. Samson. Judges 14:12
538. No
539. Solomon's temple. 1 Kings 6:7
540. Approximately eighty dollars. 2 Chronicles 1:17
541. Yes, apparently so. Deuteronomy 21:10-12
542. Job 37:10
543. Read Proverbs 30:15,16
544. Yes. James 5:14,15
545. Wafers made with honey. Exodus 16:31
546. Judas. John 12:4-6
547. Mephibosheth. 2 Samuel 4:4
548. Yes. Genesis 11:1
549. Isaiah. Isaiah 26:19
550. This word is not in the Bible.
551. Read Genesis 14:1-12
552. Joshua. Joshua 4:9
553. Joash. 2 Kings 13:14
554. Ezekiel 37:15-19
555. Sampson. Judges 13:2-5
556. Fig. Genesis 3:7
557. The "Good Samaritan." Luke 10:30-35
558. Amaziah. 2 Kings 14:17-20
559. See Exodus 2:10
560. Jehudi. Jeremiah 36:23
561. Abimelech. Judges 9:45
562. Ahab. 1 Kings 21:25
563. The children of Rechab. Jeremiah 35:1-10
564. Jeremiah. Jeremiah 32:6-9
565. Elisha. 2 Kings 4:2,3
566. No
567. White. Exodus 16:31
568. Job's. Job 16:20
569. Elisha. 2 Kings 3:14-20
570. King of Ai. Joshua 8:23-29
571. Joseph. Genesis 50:15-17
572. The Jews. Nehemiah 5:1-3
573. Twice. 1 Kings 9:2
574. Acts 19:11,12
575. God. Genesis 17:9-12
576. Yes. Job 15:12,13; Psalms 35:19
577. The children of Israel. Exodus 32:19,20
578. Samson's Judges 16:1,4,16

579. David. 2 Samuel 18:1-3
580. He fell down through a lattice in his upper chamber. 2 Kings 1:2-4,17
581. David's. Psalms 69:3
582. Isaiah. Isaiah 55:12
583. With his feet. Proverbs 6:12,13
584. Yes, apparently so. Exodus 15:8
585. Yes. Exodus 23:4,5
586. Fir. 2 Samuel 6:5
587. Isaiah. Isaiah 43:19,20
588. Nimrod and Esau. Genesis 10:8,9; Genesis 25:27
589. Twelve months. Esther 2:12,13
590. He accused them of being "brutish." Jeremiah 10:21
591. The adversaries of Judah and Benjamin. Ezra 4:1-6
592. Moses and Aaron. Exodus 7:1-7
593. Aaron and Jeroboam. Exodus 32:2-6; 1 Kings 12:26-28
594. Moab. Psalms 60:6,8
595. Acts, chapter thirteen, beginning with verse sixteen.
596. Seventy. 2 Samuel 5:4
597. Only one. 2 Kings 4:8
598. Yes. Jeremiah 23:9
599. Rebekah. Genesis 24:64-67
600. The queen of Sheba. He made 100%. 1 Kings 10:1-3
601. Uzziah. 2 Chronicles 26:9,10
602. Yes. 2 Samuel 23:1,2; Acts 1:16
603. Tertius. Romans 1:1; Romans 16:22
604. Naaman. 2 Kings 5:1-19
605. Three: 1 Kings 17:17-23; 2 Kings 4:30-37; 2 Kings 13:20,21
606. Twenty-five. Ezekiel 8:16
607. Jeremiah. Jeremiah 19:7-9
608. David. Psalms 25:6,7
609. Four: Isaac, Samson, John the Baptist, and Jesus. Genesis 18:1-10; Judges 13:2,3,24; Luke 1:13; Luke 1:26-31
610. The ostrich. Job 39:13,14
611. Forty days. Genesis 50:1-3
612. The tree of life. Revelation 22:2
613. Yes. 1 Chronicles 12:1,2
614. No

615. Jesus. Matthew 12:42
616. Four hundred. 1 Kings 18:19
617. Yes. Genesis 45:17-24
618. The. 2 Samuel 10:10
619. "Where art thou?" Genesis 3:9
620. Jair. Judges 10:3,4
621. Thirty-four
622. Jeremiah 5:3
623. Samson. Judges 14:7,8
624. Rehoboam. 2 Chronicles 11:21
625. No, a man cut it off. Judges 16:1,4,18,19
626. Proverbs 25:11
627. Yes. Isaiah 3:18-23
628. Yes. 1 Corinthians 14:34
629. Only once. Matthew 25:46
630. 1 Chronicles 4:10
631. Exodus 10:21-23
632. 1611 A. D. In making this translation possible, fifty-four scholars labored for a period of seven years.
633. She was burned to death. Judges 15:1-6
634. Shallum. 2 Kings 15:13
635. Jacob's. Genesis 31:4-7
636. No. Luke 16:22-24
637. David's. 2 Samuel 6:5
638. No, but He probably spoke the Galilean dialect of the Aramaic language.
639. Yes. Esther 2:7,20; Luke 4:16; 1 Timothy 5:10
640. Moses. Deuteronomy 34:5,6
641. Psalms 118:8
642. Genesis 1:1,2
643. The Gutenberg Bible. The present estimated value of this Bible is one million dollars.
644. Shamgar. Judges 3:31
645. No
646. Peter, James, and John. Luke 5:10,11
647. The people of Lystra. Acts 14:8-13
648. It sneezed seven times. 2 Kings 4:32-35
649. Yes. Ezekiel 37:1-10

650. In the mouth of a fish. Matthew 17:24-27
651. Azariah. 2 Kings 15:1-5
652. Yes. Song of Solomon 2:12
653. Oshea. Numbers 13:16
654. Athaliah. 2 Kings 11:13-16
655. Yes, except Ezra, Nehemiah, Esther, and Song of Solomon.
656. He requested that they wash their feet. Genesis 19:1,2
657. Only once. John 4:25,26
658. One of the editions of the King James Version contained a misprint for "vineyard" in the page heading at Luke 20, which read "Parable of the Vinegar."
659. The Geneva Bible, published in 1560 A. D.
660. Ethan, Hyman, Chalcol, and Darda. 1 Kings 4:30,31
661. During the days of Daniel. Daniel 1:11-16
662. Yes, Leviticus 7:26,27; Deuteronomy 12:23-25
663. Grinders. Ecclesiastes 12:3
664. Read Judges 2:1-4
665. Only one. Matthew 19:9
666. Nothing
667. Yes. Proverbs 25:16
668. No
669. Nehemiah. Nehemiah 5:14,15
670. Leviticus 25:10
671. On her wings. Deuteronomy 32:11
672. King Solomon. 1 Kings 10:21
673. Jesus. John 19:11
674. Some Bible students think so. Matthew 23:14; Like 12:47,48
675. The exact date is not known.
676. Yes. Leviticus 25:1-5
677. Acts of Apostles
678. Eliphaz. Job 4:15
679. Ahaz. Isaiah 38:8
680. Two angels. Genesis 19:1,2
681. Deborah. Judges 4:4,5
682. Five: Obadiah, Philemon, 2 John, 3 John, and Jude.
683. Joseph. Genesis 50:26
684. Micah. Judges 17:1,2

685. No
686. Ephesus. Acts 19:13-19
687. Forty years. Deuteronomy 29:5
688. On the eighth day Genesis 21:3,4; Luke 1:59; Luke 2:21
689. Samson. Judges 15:4,5
690. Joshua. Joshua 10:8-11
691. Yes. Psalms 22:17
692. He was born in another man's barn, Luke 2:7,16; rode on another man's beast, Matthew 21:1-11; sailed in another man's boat, Matthew 8:23-26; and was buried in another man's grave. Matthew 27:57-60 Luke 23:50-53
693. Only one time. Isaiah 34:14
694. Gossip. 1 Timothy 5:11-13
695. Yes. Jeremiah 7:30,31
696. Aaron. Numbers 20:28
697. Exodus 11:7
698. Moses, Elijah, and Jesus. Exodus 34:27,28; 1 Kings 19:1,7,8; Matthew 4:1,2
699. His enemies. 2 Corinthians 10:10
700. Judas and James. Matthew 27:3-5; Acts 12:1,2
701. David's. Psalms 39:3
702. No
703. David. 2 Samuel 11:14
704. Ezekiel 16:4
705. No
706. Ai. Joshua 7:2
707. John 21:25
708. Zerah. 2 Chronicles 14:9
709. Acts 12:10
710. Amasa. 2 Samuel 20:9,10
711. No
712. Saul. 1 Samuel, ninth and tenth chapters.
713. Hadassah. Esther 2:7
714. Five. 2 Corinthians 11:24
715. Tyrannus. Acts 19:9
716. Ezekiel. Ezekiel 30:21
717. Three. Genesis 4:1,2; Genesis 5:3,4
718. Joseph. Genesis 41-46-57
719. David's servants. 2 Samuel 10:4
720. Bath-sheba. 1 Kings 2:13
721. Athens. Acts 17:21

722. Chenaniah. 1 Chronicles 15:22
723. Tryphena and Tryphosa. Romans 16:12
724. Psalms 1:1-3
725. Judas. Matthew 27:3-5; John 12:3-6
726. Zelophehad. Numebsr 27:1-3
727. Nothing
728. Luke 23:34
729. Ezekiel. Ezekiel 8:1-3
730. Father
731. Adino. 2 Samuel 23:8
732. Job's. Job 42:12-15
733. Yes, he had a mother-in-law. Mark 1:30,31
734. Huldah's 2 Kings 22:14
735. Herod. Matthew 14:1,2
736. Strong, valiant men. 1 Samuel 14:52
737. Five. Matthew 4:18-21; Matthew 10:3
738. Men's
739. About three thousand men in one day. Exodus 32:19-28
740. Joseph of Arimathaea. Matthew 27:57-60; John 19:38
741. King Herod. Matthew 2:1-16
742. Five thousand. Acts 4:4
743. The Ephraimites. Judges 12:5,6
744. Old age. Job 42:17
745. Samson, David, and Benaiah. Judges 14:5,6; 1 Samuel 17:34-36; 1 Chronicles 11:22
746. With a bed, table, stool, and a candlestick. 2 Kings 4:9,10
747. Noah's ark. Genesis 8:1-4
748. Joseph. Genesis 47:17
749. The lion
750. In the city of Athens. Acts 17:22,23
751. One. Acts 28:16
752. Jethro. Exodus 18:13-24
753. Yes, seven. 1 Samuel 17:12
754. John, chapter seventeen.
755. Three thousand. Job 1:1,3
756. Eve. Genesis 3:1-7
757. In the sand. Exodus 2:11,12
758. John the Baptist. Luke 3:2-7
759. Three hours. Matthew 27:45,46

760. Joab. 1 Chronicles 27:34
761. Paul and Silas. Acts 17:4-6
762. Ecclesiastes 4:9
763. Hebrew
764. Yes, but only in a religious sense.
765. Simon, the Cyrenian. Mark 15:21
766. A colored man. Jeremiah 38:12,13
767. Yes. Matthew 26:26-30
768. Jacob. Genesis 35:4
769. No, but they occur more than eighty times in the New Testament.
770. Tentmaking. Acts 18:1-3
771. Yes. Matthew 16:21; Matthew 26:1,2
772. Sarah. Genesis 23:1-20
773. Yes. Matthew 5:29,30
774. Ahab. 2 Chronicles 18:3,34
775. Benjamin and Ichabod. Genesis 35:17,18; 1 Samuel 4:19-21
776. Abraham. 2 Chronicles 20:7; Isaiah 41:8; James 2:23
777. Wine. Proverbs 23:29-32
778. No
779. There is no Biblical proof that they were.
780. No
781. The love of money. 1 Timothy 6:10
782. Three: Gabriel, Michael, and Abaddon. Luke 1:13-19; Jude 1:9; Revelation 9:11
783. Nothing
784. No
785. Yes, it was published in 1917 A. D.
786. They were brothers-in-law.
787. Two. Luke 19:41; John 11:35
788. Yes
789. The sundial. 2 Kings 20:8-11
790. No, the place of Jesus' crucifixion was not called MOUNT Calvary. Luke 23:33
791. No
792. Luke 22:36
793. Certain soldiers. Luke 3:14

794. Fifty-two. Nehemiah 6:15
795. No
796. Matthew 8:21,22
797. The books of Psalms and St. John.
798. Her name is not revealed in the Bible.
799. Simon. Acts 8:13-24
800. Only one time. Isaiah 14:12
801. The name of Herodias' daughter is not definitely known.
802. About thirty. Luke 3:21-23
803. Greek
804. Yes. Exodus 15:3
805. No
806. Laban. Genesis 31:19
807. Yes. 1 Corinthians 15:33
808. Only one time. Isaiah 9:6
809. Julia Evelina Smith of Glastonbury, Connecticut, and was published in 1776 A. D. at her own expense.
810. Five: Miriam, Deborah, Huldah, Noadiah, and Anna. Exodus 15:20; Judges 4:4; 2 Kings 22:14 Nehemiah 6:14; Luke 2:36,37
811. No
812. Their names are not known.
813. Hebrews 11
814. Samuel. 1 Samuel 9:22-24
815. Isaiah 65:5
816. No
817. Ninety-nine. Genesis 17:24
818. Genesis 20:2,3
819. Elijah and Enoch. 2 Kings 2:11; Hebrews 11:5
820. Luke 24:41-43
821. Yes. Hebrews 10:24
822. Philippians 3:2
823. Samuel. 1 Samuel 3:1-9
824. A certain nobleman's. John 4:46-54
825. Deborah. Genesis 35:8
826. Jacob. Genesis 29:1-12
827. In heaven. Matthew 6:19,20
828. Read Numbers 11:1-3
829. One who meddles with strife. Proverbs 26:17

830. Those that shed innocent blood. Proverbs 6:16,17
831. Zacharias. Luke 1:5-65
832. Hiram, king of Tyre. 1 Kings 5:1-12
833. Ahab. 1 Kings 21:1-10
834. Jacob. Genesis 32:24-32
835. No
836. Elijah. 1 Kings 19:4; 2 Kings 2:1,11
837. Judas. Matthew 26:14,15;47-50
838. The Apostle Peter. Luke 22:60-62
839. Ecclesiastes 3:1,4
840. Athaliah. 2 Chronicles 24:7
841. Jacob. Genesis 37:1-4
842. Old. Matthew 9:16
843. Until death. Romans 7:1-3
844. Nebuchadnezzar. Daniel 4:33
845. No
846. The trumpet. 1 Corinthians 15:51,52
847. God's word. Psalms 119:105
848. Hebron. Genesis 23:3-20
849. King Saul. 1 Samuel 28:3-35
850. River of water of life. Revelation 22:1
851. Jacob. Genesis 25:27,28
852. Luke 14:28-30
853. Elihu. Job 32:6
854. Isaiah. Isaiah 20:3
855. Luke. Collossians 4:14
856. The anchor. Hebrews 6:19
857. Lot. Genesis 19:30
858. This word is not in the Bible.
859. Certain vineyard workers. Matthew 20:1-13
860. Abimelech. Judges 9:1-5
861. No. Proverbs 27:20
862. Deborah. Judges 4:4-14; Judges 5:1-31
863. A "tinkling" cymbal. 1 Corinthians 13:1
864. The Prophet Amos. Amos 7:14
865. The wives of Esau. Genesis 26:34,35
866. Abigail. 1 Samuel 25:18-35
867. No
868. Judges 19:22-30
869. Othniel. Judges 1:12,13

870. Pashur. Jeremiah 20:1-4
871. Yes. Deuteronomy 3:11
872. Jehu. 2 Kings 9:20
873. One time. Jeremiah 43:1,2
874. Eli. 1 Samuel 4:15,18
875. Asa. 2 Chronicles 16:12
876. He cannot lie. Hebrews 6:18
877. Only once. Colossians 2:8
878. Miriam. Numbers 12:10
879. She was his great-aunt. Exodus 6:20
880. Vashti. Esther 1:1-22
881. Priscilla. Acts 18:1-3
882. No
883. David. Psalms 116:11
884. Reuben. Genesis 49:3,4
885. Numbers 7
886. Jesus. Luke 5:3; Luke 8:22-25
887. The helm. James 3:4,5
888. There is no such book in the Bible.
889. Read John 19:23,24
890. It ran over. Psalms 23:5
891. Itching. 2 Timothy 4:3,4
892. David. 1 Samuel 17:50-54
893. Only two. Matthew 7:24-27
894. Leprosy. Leviticus 13:9-11
895. No. 1 Corinthians 7:39
896. James. Acts 12:1,2
897. Jael. Judges 4:18-22
898. Rehoboam. 2 Chronicles 11:21
899. Jehoram. 2 Chronicles 21:16-20
900. Methuselah. Genesis 5:27
901. Absalom. 2 Samuel 13:1-29
902. Elah. 1 Kings 16:8-10
903. Micah's mother. Judges 17:1-3
904. Jezebel. 1 Kings 21:5-9
905. Jeremiah. Lamentations 2:11
906. Sennacherib, king of Assyria. 2 Kings 19:36,37
907. No
908. One million five hundred and seventy thousand. 1 Chronicles 21:5
909. Eighteen
910. Zaccheus. Luke 19:1-4
911. Moab and Ben-ammi. Genesis 19:30-38
912. Yes. Galatians 5:3,4

913. Only one time. John 17:3
914. Nadab and Abihu. Leviticus 10:1,2
915. No. 1 Samuel 13:19-21
916. Amasa. 2 Samuel 20:9,10
917. Exodus 2:1-10
918. Peter, Paul, and John. Luke 22:62; Philippians 3:18; Revelation 5:4
919. Eighteen hundred and sixty-four.
920. Joash. 2 Kings 11:1-3
921. Naomi, Orpah, and Ruth. Ruth 1:3-9
922. Jesus. John 19:23
923. Yes. 2 Samuel 19:18
924. John the Baptist. Matthew 14:6-12
925. Nehemiah. Nehemiah 13:23-25
926. Tertullus. Acts 24:1
927. Rizpah. 2 Samuel 21:8-10
928. Jacob. Genesis 34:30
929. Esau. Genesis 26:34; Genesis 36:2-5
930. Uzzah. 2 Samuel 6:6,7
931. Yes. Job 1:1
932. Yes. Deuteronomy 23:24
933. Simeon. Luke 2:25-29
934. Asahel. 2 Samuel 2:18
935. Saul. 1 Samuel 9:1,2
936. An incurable disease of the bowels. 2 Chronicles 21:16-19
937. A woman. Genesis 31:19
938. Only one time. 1 Timothy 5:23
939. Hannah. 1 Samuel 1:12-15
940. Ezra. Nehemiah 8:4
941. Dorcas. Acts 9:36-39
942. Ehud. Judges 3:15
943. Zelophehad's. Numbers 27:1-11
944. Joseph. Genesis 43:30,31
945. Tahpenes. 1 Kings 11:19,20
946. A yoke. Jeremiah 28:10
947. Job's wife. Job 2:7-9
948. Noah. Genesis 9:20,21; 2 Peter 2:5
949. Abraham. Genesis 21:8
950. Rachel. Genesis 29:9
951. Absalom. 2 Samuel 14:25
952. No
953. Lot. 2 Peter 2:7,8

954. Jabez's 1 Chronicles 4:9
955. Jacob. Genesis 27:11
956. Huldah. 2 Chronicles 34:22
957. Ahab. 1 Kings 21:2-4
958. Daniel. Daniel 6:2
959. There is no such book in the Bible.
960. Caleb. Joshua 14:6-11
961. Eli. 1 Samuel 4:15,18
962. Eglon. Judges 3:17
963. Samson's. Judges 14:16,17
964. Zipporah. Exodus 4:25
965. Haman. Esther 7:10
966. Baruch. Jeremiah 36:10,17,18
967. Goliath. 1 Samuel 17:4
968. Jubal. Genesis 4:21
969. Leah. Genesis 29:17
970. Michal. 2 Samuel 6:16
971. Jezebel. 2 Kings 9:30-34
972. Esau and Elijah. Genesis 27:11; 2 Kings 1:7,8
973. Joshua. Joshua 1:1,8
974. Her name is not known.
975. Ahithophel. 2 Samuel 17:23
976. Issachar. Genesis 49:14
977. Jeroboam. 1 Kings 11:28
978. Ishmael. Genesis 16:11
979. Hanun. 1 Chronicles 19:4
980. Gideon. Judges 8:30,31
981. Laban. Genesis 29:21-30
982. Joseph. Genesis 41:14
983. "It is more blessed to give than to receive." Acts 20:35
984. Sarah. Genesis 17:17,19; Genesis 21:1,2
985. Yes, except fifty-five verses.
986. Yes. Revelation 1:11
987. No
988. Barak. Judges 4:4-9
989. Belshazzar. Daniel 5:1,6
990. No. Leviticus 14:1-32
991. Mary Magdalene. Mark 16:9; Luke 8:1,2
992. Esau. Genesis 25:29-34
993. Jehoiakim, king of Judah. Jeremiah 36:30
994. Jerusalem. Zephaniah 1:12
995. No, it was a Roman punishment.
996. King of Egypt. 2 Kings 17:4

85

997. No, it means *so be it.*
998. Gideon's soldiers. Judges 7:15,16
999. Saul. 1 Samuel 11:6,7
1000. Ben-hadad. 2 Kings 8:7,15
1001. No
1002. 1 Corinthians 15
1003. See Deuteronomy 14:21
1004. Jared. Genesis 5:20
1005. Nebuchadnezzar. Daniel 4:33
1006. Thirty-six
1007. Numbers 11:5
1008. The Ten Commandments
1009. 1 Kings 13:20-24
1010. Bread
1011. Saul's. 1 Samuel 31:4-10
1012. No
1013. Paul. Philippians 4:2
1014. Jehoiachin. Jeremiah 52:31-34
1015. Hiram. 1 Kings 9:11-13
1016. Cain. Genesis 4:13
1017. The spider. Proverbs 30:28
1018. Jehoiakim. Jeremiah 22:18,19
1019. 2 Chronicles 36:22,23
1020. Micah. Judges 17:10-13
1021. Abdon. Judges 12:13,14
1022. Jotham. Judges 9:21
1023. Benaiah. 1 Chronicles 11:22
1024. Melchisedec. Hebrews 7:1-3
1025. Pharaoh. Genesis 47:8
1026. Obadiah. 1 Kings 18:4
1027. Yes. Acts 19:29-31
1028. Boaz. Ruth 4:5-10
1029. Yes. Exodus 21:28
1030. Zimri. 1 Kings 16:15-18
1031. Hosea 4:13
1032. Eutychus. Acts 20:7-9
1033. 2 Kings 12:9-11
1034. The first six books of the Old Testament.
1035. David. 1 Kings 2:10
1036. David. Amos 6:5
1037. Baruch. Jeremiah 36:18
1038. Ibzan. Judges 12:8,9
1039. Jeremiah 25:34
1040. Nehemiah. Nehemiah 2:11-16
1041. Thirteen. 1 Kings 7:1
1042. Yes. Deuteronomy 33:4,5
1043. Agabus. Acts 21:10,11
1044. Yes. Jonah 4:5-7

1045. Gideon. Judges 8:22,23
1046. Yes. Malachi 3:8,9
1047. Jonah. Jonah 4:8
1048. Isaiah 19:10
1049. Herod. Luke 13:31,32
1050. Daniel. Daniel 5:29
1051. Cain. Genesis 4:13,14
1052. Three times. Acts 17:29; Romans 1:20; Colossians 2:9
1053. Genesis 31:43-46
1054. Eden. Genesis 2:8
1055. Genesis 3:15
1056. Exodus 22:29
1057. Amos. Amos 7:14
1058. Mephibosheth. 2 Samuel 9:6-8
1059. David. 2 Samuel 11:1-27
1060. Lot. Genesis 14:1-16
1061. Jonathan. 1 Samuel 14:24,27,43, 45
1062. Eli. 1 Samuel 1:12,13
1063. Abraham. Genesis 21:22-24
1064. Barzillai. 2 Samuel 19:34-37
1065. Zebulun. 1 Chronicles 12:33
1066. Genesis 28:22
1067. Jehoiachin. 2 Chronicles 36:9
1068. Ahaz. 2 Chronicles 28:24
1069. Joseph. Genesis 37:28
1070. Abraham. Genesis 12:1-3
1071. Rebekah. Genesis 27:46
1072. Achan. Joshua 7:24-26
1073. Moses and Joshua. Exodus 3:4,5; Joshua 5:15
1074. Amos
1075. Numbers 31:22
1076. Solomon. 1 Kings 2:19-25
1077. Hezekiah. 2 Kings 18:1,4
1078. See Exodus 21:18,19
1079. Hezekiah. 2 Kings 20:1
1080. Araunah. 2 Samuel 24:23
1081. David. 2 Samuel 24:14
1082. Isaiah
1083. Hagar. Genesis 21:14-16
1084. Beor. Joshua 13:22
1085. Sarah. Genesis 12:10-14
1086. Augustus Caesar. Luke 2:1
1087. Gamaliel. Acts 5:34
1088. Rehoboam. 1 Kings 12:6-8
1089. Paul. 1 Corinthians 15:9
1090. Elijah. 1 Kings 17:1-6

1091. Philip. Acts 21:8
1092. A certain deaf man. Mark 7:31-35
1093. Moses. Mark 9:2-5
1094. Yes. Mark 10:27
1095. Meeknes. Numbers 12:3
1096. Alexander. 2 Timothy 4:14
1097. The soul of man. Matthew 16:26
1098. Zacharias. Luke 1:13-23
1099. During the reign of King Solomon. 2 Chronicles 1:13-15
1100. Babylon. Isaiah 13:19,20
1101. Yes. Deuteronomy 2:6
1102. Nathan-melch. 2 Kings 23:11
1103. Love. Song of Solomon 8:7
1104. Yes. Isaiah 55:7; Ezekiel 18:20,21
1105. Seer. 1 Samuel 9:9
1106. Pharisees. Acts 26:1-5
1107. Seven days. Numbers 19:11
1108. Abner. 2 Samuel 3:37,38
1109. They have sinned in the past. 2 Peter 2:4; Jude 1:6
1110. Deborah. Genesis 35:8
1111. This word is not in the Bible.
1112. Moses. Exodus 3:4,5
1113. Yes. Exodus 33:17-20
1114. Judges 10:7
1115. Solomon. 2 Samuel 12:24
1116. Jephthah's daughter. Judges 11:30-40
1117. Forty days. Acts 1:1-3
1118. "Remember the Sabbath day, to keep it holy." Exodus 20:8
1119. Troas. Acts 20:7-9
1120. Cain. Genesis 4:8,9
1121. Luke
1122. Dinah. Genesis 30:17-21
1123. When the seventh seal was opened there was silence for about "half an hour." Revelation 8:1
1124. Approximately eighteen inches. Judges 3:16-25
1125. Because of the corrupt government of Samuel's sons. 1 Samuel 8:1-5
1126. About a whole day. Joshua 10:12,13

1127. Yes. Judges 5:29
1128. Three thousand. Judges 16:27-30
1129. The men of Succoth. Judges 8:4-6
1130. In the days of the Prophet Samuel. 1 Samuel 12:16-19
1131. Hewers of wood and drawers of water. Joshua 9:3,23
1132. With a file. 1 Samuel 13:19-21
1133. Cursed. Joshua 6:26
1134. No
1135. A coat of many colors. Genesis 37:3
1136. This word is not in the Bible.
1137. About forty years old. Acts 4:1-22
1138. Seven times each day. Psalms 119:164
1139. "Stranger" and "sojourner." Psalms 39:12
1140. A shock of corn in its season. Job 5:26
1141. Seventeen years old. Genesis 37:2-36
1142. An offended brother. Proverbs 18:19
1143. David. 1 Chronicles 29:26-28
1144. The Laodicean church. Revelation 3:14.15
1145. Seventy years. Jeremiah 25:11,-12
1146. A gourd. Jonah 4:6-10
1147. Seven days. Ezekiel 3:15
1148. A lost sheep. Psalms 119:176
1149. Abraham. Genesis 22:1-14
1150. One thousand. Daniel 5:1
1151. Jehu, he drove "furiously." 2 Kings 9:20
1152. The queen of Sheba. 1 Kings 10:1
1153. No
1154. David. 1 Kings 2:1,2
1155. Forty-six years. John 2:20
1156. 1 Chronicles 2:34,35
1157. 1 Kings 10:22
1158. No
1159. Jerusalem. Lamentations 2:10
1160. Genesis 26:12

1161. Because he was the son of his old age. Genesis 37:3
1162. Genesis 13:14
1163. No
1164. Mount Moriah. 2 Chronicles 3:1
1165. Joseph. Genesis 37:3,4
1166. This disease is not mentioned by name in the Bible.
1167. Hill of Samaria. 1 Kings 16:23,24
1168. Matthew 27:29
1169. Nineveh. Nahum 3:7-10
1170. Numbers 21:17-20
1171. Death. Deuteronomy 21:18-21
1172. Second John
1173. The Hebrew nation, or Israelites. Exodus 12:31-36
1174. Six years. Exodus 21:2
1175. Only one. Acts 16:14
1176. Thirty days. Deuteronomy 34:8
1177. Jerusalem, the city of David 2 Samuel 5:6-9
1178. Jezebel. 2 Kings 9:30-34
1179. Death. Leviticus 24:16
1180. No
1181. Yes. John 2:13-15
1182. Proverbs 20:1
1183. Pride. Proverbs 16:18
1184. Yes. Isaiah 14:12; Isaiah 29:1
1185. David. Luke 2:4
1186. Four: Matthew 4:18-22
1187. Jacob. Genesis 32:9,10
1188. Anna, the prophetess. Luke 2:36,37
1189. No
1190. The Elamites. Jeremiah 49:36
1191. Yes. Isaiah 1:3
1192. The cave at Makkedah. Joshua 10:15-17
1193. Pashur. Jeremiah 20:1-3
1194. Hezekiah. Isaiah 38:2
1195. Daniel. Daniel 1:17
1196. In the Garden of Eden. Genesis 3:8-19
1197. Paul. Hebrews 12:21
1198. Numbers 5:22
1199. This word is not in the Scriptures.
1200. Manasseh. 2 Kings 21:18

1201. Acts of Apostles, chapter twenty-seven.
1202. Agur. Proverbs 30:1,8
1203. No
1204. David, by Shimei. 2 Samuel 16:5-8
1205. Ruth. Ruth 1:16
1206. Jezebel. 2 Kings 9:30-37
1207. Elkanah. 1 Samuel 1:8
1208. Hadadezer. 2 Samuel 8:3,4
1209. Psalms
1210. Abimelech. Judges 9:45-49
1211. Yes. Acts 23:1-3
1212. Deborah. Judges 4:4,5
1213. The Bible makes no mention of such.
1214. Peter. Matthew 26:69,74
1215. King Saul. 1 Samuel 16:21-23
1216. Twice: Exodus, chapter twenty, and Deuteronomy, chapter five.
1217. Turns away wrath. Proverbs 15:1
1218. A certain Pharisee. Luke 18:11
1219. Bad. Luke 6:26
1220. This word is not in the Scriptures.
1221. Judges 9:8-15
1222. Yes. 2 Timothy 3:16,17; 2 Peter 1:20,21
1223. Five. 1 Samuel 17:38-40
1224. Yes. Matthew 17:24-27
1225. Four: He "went about doing good." Acts 10:38
1226. Death. Romans 6:23
1227. No. 1 Corinthians 10:13
1228. The Apostle Paul, First Corinthians, chapter fifteen.
1229. No
1230. John 20:1-9
1231. Yes, one time. Leviticus 25:5
1232. Because Saint Luke was a physician. Colossians 4:14
1233. No
1234. Jesus. Luke 10:7
1235. Yes. Proverbs 19:17; Luke 6:38
1236. Any time. Matthew 24:36-44
1237. "The righteous forsaken, nor His seed begging bread." Psalms 37:25

1238. He hanged himself. Matthew 27:3-5
1239. Tarsus. Acts 21:39
1240. Psalms 103:16
1241. No. James 1:13
1242. Righteousness. Proverbs 14:34
1243. Pilate. Matthew 27:17-25
1244. This word is not in the Bible.
1245. Yes. James 2:19
1246. God. Genesis 3:19
1247. Jethro. Exodus 18:7,8
1248. No. John 18:31
1249. Approximately sixteen hundred.
1250. Jacob. Genesis 27:1-29
1251. Only one time. Joel 3:4
1252. Joshua. Zechariah 3:1-3
1253. Yes, one time each. Psalms 105:21,22; Acts 5:21
1254. Rebekah. Genesis 24:61-67
1255. Jacob. Genesis 47:29
1256. Zedekiah. 1 Kings 22:24
1257. Lazarus. John 11:11-44
1258. Jacob. Genesis 28:10,11
1259. No
1260. Paul's nephew. Acts 23:12-35
1261. Moses. Deuteronomy 34:7
1262. Sackcloth. 2 Samuel 3:31
1263. No
1264. See Acts 1:7,8
1265. Jesus. Matthew 4:1-10
1266. Wheat, barley, and corn.
1267. Acts 19:1-7
1268. No
1269. Samson. Judges 14:12
1270. Raven. Genesis 8:6,7
1271. James and Jude
1272. Eve. Genesis 3:20
1273. No. Mark 12:18-25
1274. Mulberry. 2 Samuel 5:22-25
1275. Manasseh, fifty-five years. 2 Chronicles 33:1
1276. Isaiah
1277. Some Bible students think so. Matthew 18:10; Hebrews 1:13,14
1278. No. Genesis 8:21,22; Genesis 9:9-17
1279. Methuselah. Genesis 5:26-29

1280. "Father, forgive them; they know not what they do." Luke 23:34
1281. The leopard. Jeremiah 13:23
1282. 1488 A. D.
1283. Yes. Amos 4:7
1284. King Saul. 2 Samuel 1:17-19
1285. Only one step. 1 Samuel 20:3
1286. No. Jeremiah 23:24
1287. The human heart. Jeremiah 17:9
1288. Only one time. Psalms 111:9
1289. The "Good Samaritan." Luke 10:30-37
1290. No. Leviticus 11:4
1291. Rahab. Joshua 2:1-22
1292. Goat. Matthew 25:31-46
1293. Five thousand shekels of brass. 1 Samuel 17:4,5
1294. No. Isaiah 45:18,19
1295. Saul and Jonathan. 2 Samuel 1:23
1296. Trumpets of rams' horns. Joshua 6:6-20
1297. A double portion of an inheritance. Deuteronomy 21:17
1298. The Jews. Numbers 11:4,5
1299. Peter's. Matthew 8:14
1300. No, they had to wait one month. Deuteronomy 21:11-14
1301. The lily. Matthew 6:28,29
1302. Sapphira. Acts 5:1-10
1303. Bethlehem. Luke 2:4-7
1304. No
1305. Asshur. Genesis 10:11
1306. No, quotation marks were not in use when the King James Translation of the Bible was printed in 1611 A. D.
1307. Yes, they were cousins. Luke 1:26-60
1308. Isaiah 53:3
1309. Yes. Proverbs 30:28
1310. Lydia. Acts 16:14,15
1311. Yes, one time. Numbers 5:17
1312. David. 2 Samuel 12:15-23
1313. Yes. John 1:45; John 6:42
1314. Esther 8:9
1315. Seven hundred. Judges 20:14-16

89

1316. A meek and quiet spirit. 1 Peter 3:1-4
1317. No
1318. Matthew 25
1319. A renewal of strength. Isaiah 40:31
1320. No
1321. Only one time. Acts 7:56
1322. Asahel, Abner, Ishbosheth, and Amasa. 2 Samuel 2:22,23 2 Samuel 3:27; 2 Samuel 4:5,6; 2 Samuel 20:10
1323. Seven. Adam, Seth, Enos, Cainan, Jared, Methuselah, and Noah.
1324. 46,227
1325. Agag, king of the Amalekites. 1 Samuel 15:32,33
1326. Matthew. Matthew 9:9
1327. 1881 A. D.
1328. Yes
1329. Ephraim. Hosea 7:8
1330. Moses. Numbers 32:23
1331. The child Ichabod. 1 Samuel 4:16-20
1332. Forty-nine
1333. Keturah. Genesis 25:1
1334. Achan. Joshua 7:19-25
1335. Michal. 2 Samuel 6:20-23
1336. Balaam. Numbers 22:28,29
1337. Hananiah. Jeremiah 28:15-17
1338. Straight. Acts 9:10,11
1339. The Apostle Paul. Acts 21:37
1340. Vophsi, Vashni, and Vashti. Numbers 13:14; 1 Chronicles 6:28; Esther 1:9
1341. 1901 A.D.
1342. No
1343. No
1344. 1 Kings 19:12
1345. Babylon. Matthew 1:11
1346. Psalms 117
1347. Sarah and Anna. Genesis 23:1; Luke 2:36, 37
1348. Moses. Exodus 32:15-19
1349. Ezekiel. Ezekiel 24:1-14
1350. Thirty-three
1351. No
1352. The Apostle Paul. Acts 26:19-25

1353. Ahithophel. 2 Samuel 15:12
1354. Ruth. Ruth 2:8-14
1355. Psalms 119
1356. Absalom. 2 Samuel 14:25
1357. Pilate's wife. Matthew 27:19
1358. A certain widow's son. 1 Kings 17:17-23
1359. Abishai. 2 Samuel 23:18
1360. Ahab. 1 Kings 21:28, 29
1361. Jeremiah 32:9-15
1362. Solomon. 1 Kings 10:16, 18
1363. Mount Sinai. Exodus 34:1-3
1364. The Apostle Paul's. Acts 23:12, 13
1365. No
1366. Samson. Judges 16:30, 31
1367. The Gibeonites. Joshua 9:3-15
1368. The Prophet Elijah. 1 Kings 19:1-8
1369. Jethro, his father-in-law. Exodus 18:5-7
1370. An Egyptian. 1 Samuel 30:9-13
1371. Two hundred and sixty
1372. No
1373. Jeremiah. Jeremiah 30:5, 6
1374. The Prophet Elijah. 2 Kings 1:3, 8
1375. Yes. Genesis 26:34, 35
1376. Proverbs 31:10-31
1377. Judah. Genesis 49:8-11
1378. This word is not in the New Testament.
1379. 117
1380. Abraham and Sarah. Genesis 25:8-10
1381. No
1382. Yes. Proverbs 6:13
1383. A personality. Matthew 4:1-11; Matthew 25:41
1384. Jacob. Genesis 48:3-10
1385. Jephthah. Judges 11:1; Judges 12:7
1386. Lot's wife. Genesis 19:23-26
1387. Paul. 2 Corinthians 11:25
1388. The Cretians. Titus 1:12
1389. Amos. Amos 8:9
1390. Stephen. Acts 6:8-15; Acts 7:1-60
1391. Herod. Acts 12:21-23

1392. Death. Exodus 31:14
1393. Jehu. 2 Kings 9:24
1394. The daughters of Lot. Genesis 19:30-38
1395. Malchus. John 18:10
1396. Seventy-one

1397. Abijah. 2 Chronicles 13:21
1398. Balaam's ass. Numbers 22:21-23
1399. The wife of Phinehas. 1 Samuel 4:19-21
1400. This question cannot be answered with certainty.

QUIZ AND PUZZLE BOOKS

Bible Acrostics, by W. Smith
Bible-Centered Crossword Puzzles,
  by C. E. Whitlow
Bible Clue Puzzle Book,
  by W. P. Keasbey
Bible Crossword Puzzle Book,
  by S. K. Davis
Bible Dial-a-Word, by G. DeYoung
Bible Facts in Crossword Puzzles,
  by F. Spencer
Bible Facts the Easy Way, by E. Filipi
Bible Key Word Quizzes,
  by J. G. Malphurs
Bible Number Quiz Book, by M. Stilson
Bible People in Crossword Puzzles,
  No. 2, by L. P. Johnson
Bible Puzzles for Adults,
  by G. Vander Klay
Bible Puzzles, Quizzes and Games,
  by H. Pettigrew
Bible Questions in Rhymes, Puzzles,
  Quizzes and Games, by M. O. Honors
Bible Quiz Book, by F. Hall
Bible Quizzes and Puzzles,
  by H. Pettigrew
Bible Quizzes for Everybody, by F. Hall
Bible, Quizzes, Jumbles, and Matches,
  by A. Ford
Bible Stories in Acrostic Puzzles,
  by S. Smith
Bible Word Quest, by H. Pettigrew
Bible Word Search, by W. C. Gordon
Build a Word Bible Puzzles,
  by M. Stilson
Creation Story in Acrostic Puzzles,
  by S. Smith
Criss Crossword Puzzles of Bible,
  by D. W. Thompson
Crossword Puzzles from Bible Verses,
  by Paul N. Jones
1500 Bible Quizzes, by A. R. Wells
1400 Bible Facts, by E. C. McKenzie

Go Till You Guess, by A. R. Wells
Intriguing Bible Puzzles,
  by Erma Reynolds
Know Your Bible Better Quiz Book,
  by F. Hall
Know Your Bible Quiz Book,
  by A. R. Wells
Know Your Hymns Quiz Book
  by F. Hall
Life of Christ in Crossword Puzzles,
  by L. P. Johnson
Miracles and Parables of the Bible in
  Crossword Puzzles, by L. P. Johnson
New Testament in Crossword Puzzles,
  by L. P. Johnson
Number Quizzes on the Bible,
  by V. Hutchcroft
Old Testament in Crossword Puzzles,
  by L. P. Johnson
Puzzle Fun with Bible Clues,
  by W. P. Keasbey
Quickie Quizzes from the Bible 1,
  by C. Vander Meer
Quickie Quizzes from Bible 2,
  by C. Vander Meer
Quiz Book on the Bible, by A. W. Kelly
Scripture-Based Crossword Puzzles,
  by G. Whitlow
Scripture Geometrics,
  by Jeffrey L. Fullman
Seek and Find Bible Puzzles,
  by M. Stilson
Teaching of Bible in Crossword Puzzles,
  by L. P. Johnson
Teachings of Christ in Crossword
  Puzzles, by L. P. Johnson
What Do You Know? Bible Quizzes,
  by V. Pewtress
When? Why? How? Bible Quizzes,
  by M. Stilson
Who? What? Where? Bible Quizzes,
  by M. Stilson

BAKER BOOK HOUSE
Grand Rapids, Michigan